I Saw God Along the Way

Stories of God's Faithfulness, Kindness, and Protection

JOY KEATING GULICK

Copyright © 2018 Joy Gulick

All rights reserved.

ISBN:
ISBN-13:978-1981500086
ISBN-10-1981500081

DEDICATION

How can I give thanks enough to my husband, Roger, and my brother, Paul Keating, who have encouraged me to tell my stories of what God has done throughout my life and along the way. Their help has been a sheer gift of time, energy and love.

INTRODUCTION

At times I've missed the subtle touch of God along the way. God's touch is gentle and often unnoticed in the rush of life. I'm often too busy and distracted to realize it's Him. So, I've written this book to say, "Thank you, Lord for all your care and surprises along the way, and for the joy you have always brought even though I was too busy to notice."

I trust that because of this book you will become increasingly aware of His loving touch in your life. Space has been left at the bottom of each story for you to jot down something of those times when you saw, or felt, or sensed God's touch in your life.

> As I look back over my life I have
>
> seen God's love, faithfulness, and
>
> incredible ways of dealing with me.
>
> Ways that aren't at all what I
>
> would have expected, but oh, so
>
> good!
>
> > Good for me,
> >
> > Good for His kingdom,
> >
> > Good for others,
> >
> > Some   dramatic,
> >
> > Some   surprising
> >
> > Some frightening
> >
> > But in the end so good!

I SAW GOD ALONG THE WAY

CONTENTS

1	FROM RUSSIA WITH LOVE	Pg. 1
2	SLEUTHS IN THE NIGHT	Pg 5
3	AN EXCITING OPPORTUNITY	Pg 11
4	A NEW SMILE	Pg 16
5	AN INCREDIBLE SURPRISE	Pg 19
6	DOUGLAS NORMAN	Pg 22
7	IT HAPPENED AT MACDONALDS	Pg 26
8	WE'RE RUNNING OUT OF MONEY	Pg 29
9	HERE'S TO AUNT HELEN	Pg 32
10	MAXIMO	Pg 35
11	AN UNEXPECTED HELP	Pg 38
12	EMPTY GAS TANK	Pg 40
13	A CURIOUS HAPPENING	Pg 44
14	TENNIS ANYONE	Pg 51
15	THE GREEN MAMBA	Pg 54
16	AN STRANGE HELP	Pg 62
17	ANGELS?	Pg 65
18	A SPECIL GIFT	Pg 69
19	HOW WILL I GET HOME	Pg 73

20	A TURNING POINT	Pg 76
21	ALONE	Pg 79
22	JOHN HAMPTON EDDIE	Pg 84
23	GOD WORKS ALL THINGS FOR GOOD	Pg 88
24	THE LIE	Pg 90
25	THE "WAY IINN"	Pg 95
26	BEYONG EXPECTATIONS	Pg 100
27	A KNOCK AT MY DOOR	Pg 104
28	I'LL TAKE SIX, BUT NO MEALS	Pg 108
29	WOOD CHIPS	Pg 112
30	OH NO!	Pg 116
31	A ROAD LESS TRAVELED	Pg 119
32	BUT FOR THIS VERY HOUR…	Pg 122
33	NOW WHAT?	Pg 126
34	A SUNBEAM	Pg 129
35	JUST IN TIME	Pg 133
36	IT WAS MORE THT THE OIL	Pg 135
37	FAMILY FORGIVENESS	Pg 138
38	ACHTUNG	Pg 141
39	GOD'S AMAZING KINDNESS	Pg 145
40	LITTLE DID I KNOW…	Pg 148

I SAW GOD ALONG THE WAY

Chapter 1

TO RUSSIA WITH LOVE

Traveling can be fun—except for: communicating, finding one's way on trains, having impossible plane schedules that make you run through five terminals, automobiles driving on the wrong side of the road, hotels with unmade rooms, and locating friends in places with perplexing languages. *Parle vou François?*

Russia is one of the hardest places to travel. None of their words or accents looks or sounds like English…or Spanish, Italian, German, Dutch or Romanian. Those languages I can sometimes decipher and partially understand, but Russian…no way.

Fortunately, our recent travel to Russia was to visit Tom and Carol, missionaries, who had lived for seven years in Krasnador in southern Russia. It was going to be a simple and fun experience. Tom and Carol would take over and translate their little hearts out for us and make it memorable.

Roger and I had just finished leading a conference in Vienna, packed and headed off to the airport. We strolled up to the ticket counter tugging our battered travel-ons; Roger looked dignified and experienced. I was worn around the edges. At the boarding desk we handed over our magnificently stamped passports that at least indicated that we'd been through the travel routine before for almost every page was filled with rubber stampings from thirty different countries.

I had begun to slump but was still smiling. The ticket agent, friendly, though stern-looking in her black tailored uniform, looked at Roger's dark blue passport, examined the Russian visa, that had cost almost $200 and briskly stamped it and produced a boarding pass.

Fighting major fatigue, I forced myself to the counter put on my most charming, glistening American smile. The attendant awarded me a cursory glance--she in her black uniform—then crisply said, "I'm sorry, but your visa has expired."

"What? That can't be! Roger, do something." He looked at the document, while being as perplexed as I. But sure enough, the visa date had expired just the week before our travel. (Truth be told; I was momentarily delighted that it was not *my* mistake. I never dealt well with the intricacies of bureaucratic details. That was way above my pay grade.) Well, it turned out that *Roger*, my loving, detail checker, had clicked the wrong month on his computer screen when he filled out the Russian visa application.

"God, now what?" In a couple hours we're supposed to fly to Moscow and then Krasnador. We can't now. How are we supposed to change our whole schedule and tickets? The airline agent, still in her stiff black uniform, commented that if she let me go into Russia, I would be fined $500 dollars, or rubles, or any of that funny money. "Vee vud be sent back to Austria on the next flight…at our own expense!" (We don't need to be in Austria. We need to be in Russia!) Then she said in her convincing accent. "Ah vud provably looze mine yob eef I leaf you go… Next?" Well that was it. I was in shock.

While I was trying to keep my panic meter on neutral, it occurred to me that God must still have something for us to do here in Vienna—or, given our world, He was protecting us from some unimaginable, headline-making crises in Russia.

As we dejectedly walked down the long, dreary gray terminal hall, wondering whatever to do next, we were surprised to run into the Wrights. They were missionary couple we knew who had faithfully worked in Central Europe for years. We all hugged and told them our embarrassing story. They explained that they'd just gotten back to the country. They knew we had been in Vienna for the conference, but they had been working in Romania. "We had been praying that we could talk to you before you left the area. We've been going through a difficult time and needed a listening ear and some counsel."

"OK, Lord, I get it," I thought."

We found a coffee shop and had an hour to talk through some of their concerns before they were to be picked up. Somewhere at the end of a meaningful discussion that ended with tears and praise, we told them about the visa mix up that made it possible for us to have time with them, "We're *supposed to be* in route to Krasnador for six days and then to Jordan to see another staff couple for a few days—but we're a week early for that."

As we were speaking and puzzling over what we were to do, another of our missionary couples walked in. They had come to pick up the couple we had been talking with. More embraces. We shared our latest episodes and laughed and spoke of our amazement at how things worked out to have time with the Wrights. But our schedule was still really messed up. They invited us to their home for the night.

We were exhilarated by the way God had provided. Yet, something was brewing. Since it was a week early for us to travel to our missionary's home in Jordan, we made some quick phone calls to see if we could arrive early. "Sure, sure, that'll be great." Now we only needed to change our tickets. We already had our visas. The next morning it was *off to Jordan!* I slept the whole flight to Amman.

During our first day in Jordan, we received an e-mail from our Russian missionaries: "My father has just died, and we have to leave right away for the States for the funeral." Hmm, God's plan. What if we had gone to Russia? Well, we would have been stuck in Krasnador for days where we knew not a soul or the language or have any reason to be there because our team members were gone to care for their grieving family.

Thank you, Lord for taking our mistakes and making something good out of them.

"The Lord is my Shepherd; I shall not want." Psalm 23.

YOUR STORY OF A MISTAKE THAT GOD USED.

_____
_____
_____
_____
_____

Chapter 2

SLEUTHS IN THE NIGHT

If you have been reading from page one, you will have discovered that I am not basically a brave person, and I probably have an over active imagination about what could happen in situations where I don't have much control. There is a lot of approach –avoidance I feel in new challenging situations. My best plan in new situations is to sit back and observe for a while and when I think everything is safe I'll risk entering in to whatever is going on. With those words as a back drop, I will tell my next story.

A missionary friend of my husband and mine asked us if we would be willing to go in to Communist Romania. This was in 1986 before the Iron Curtain was down. He wanted Roger to teach untrained church leaders in several towns throughout Romania. We would go as tourists and end up in private homes where these men clandestinely would come to be trained for leadership in underground churches. It sounded scary, but also wonderful to be able to impact a country by training those who were trying to lead in their churches.

We were to arrive in Vienna after we had just been in Africa for two weeks. David, a missionary to Romania, would meet us there and lead us into the country. We took a train from Vienna to Budapest and then a flight to Bucharest. I wasn't too nervous because David was a pro at international ministry and had been in the country many times. In fact, he had lived in Romania for two years on a Fulbright scholarship to study the language.

As the plane was about to land in Bucharest, David so very quietly said to us, "If I can't get through passport control, (Often people would get black listed for no reason at all.) get a bus to a certain square in the city, walk down two blocks from the square and turn left on to a little street and half way down the block on the right there will be a church. It doesn't look like a church. It is a small and drab house, but it has a cross on the gate. Go there and tell them Paul sent you." That was the false name he used in country. What! In my heart I was thinking, "Are you kidding! We don't know the language. What if we get lost, what if…, what if…?"

We were to go through separate lines through pass port control. At this point I'm looking at Roger and saying, "I'm not sure we should do this." Roger just gave this look like "I guess we have to; this is why we came." I wasn't so sure. We are going to end up in prison. I had this rush of approach avoidance. I wanted to say, NO! But then there was this other very little part of me that said, "I will die for Christ if necessary."

Roger and I both made it through passport control and we frantically looked around for David. "Look Roger, he made it!" What a relief. Later as we took the path he suggested to the little church, both Roger and I said to each other, "We would never have found the church by ourselves." It was a dilapidated old wooden house behind a dark unpainted dilapidated fence. Thank you, Lord, David made it through passport control.

David neglected to tell me to bring my drabbest of drab clothes, so I would just blend in with all the very dark and dreary looking people of the country. I arrived in an African dress of purple and gold with little purple sandals with thin straps wrapped around my ankles. I looked like a head light in this very dark country. So much for my fading into the back ground.

Romania was a country where there were not many people out on the streets. In the capital not only were there not many people out on the streets but it might be several minutes before a car might pass by. When one walked by people, they rarely looked up and a smile was never on their face. As we spent more time in Romania we were struck very strongly by the dysfunction of about everything we saw. Often the toilets had to have a bucket of water thrown down them to get them to flush. The towels in the average hotel we stayed at looked like one of your dish towels that had been used for twenty years.

At night in an eight-story building there might only be one light bulb hanging in the stair well. The elevators sometimes didn't work, or they would get stuck half way up, and we would have to crawl out through a crack in the elevator door that the men would have to pull open. (Not my favorite elevator experiences.) We would walk forever to find a place that had any food. Remember this was a major city. Once in a city of several hundred thousand we walked for an hour before we found a restaurant that was open. The food was awful, to the point of not wanting to eat it. I ordered ice cream thinking they could not possibly ruin ice cream. Wrong! It was like Crisco with milk on it. I still can feel the grease in my mouth. Bad! Local people were not to talk with foreigners without reporting it to the police and that rule was enforced. So here we were breaking all the rules of contact with the nationals. We were like sleuths in the night.

One story gives a clue to the length one would have to go to protect the Christian Romanians from imprisonment or a steep fine. We were now registered in a large hotel. About a day after we registered at the hotel, we were assigned a Securitate agent (secret police) who was to follow us without us knowing. Being a good body language reader, I thought I spotted a man who was acting a little strange at the door of the hotel, so I bravely went up and stood next to him and looked at him, so he realized I had seen his face. He quickly went flying out the door on to the main street, not to be seen for a while.

His story to be continued.

David said we needed to do some tourist stuff around town, so we didn't look obvious. Who would ever really want to tour there? We walked around stores that were almost vacant with few things to buy. Then we took a tour boat down the river to the next town where we were to meet our first contact. David said," When you get off the boat, walk slowly and act like a tourist. A man will meet us who will tell us where to go next." I was now into detective training 101. We started walking and David said, "I see him, now just walk slowing past him and he will tell us what time we are to meet him for the first meeting". I had no idea how clandestine this journey would be. It was kind of fun and exciting. James Bond had nothing on us. As the man walked by David he quickly said, "Six o'clock in front of the Delta Hotel. We walked on past him without even looking at him.

We acted like tourist for an hour until we saw our contact in front of the hotel. David said, "Walk slowly toward the end of the building. We did, and when we turned the corner there was a car waiting for us with the doors open. Anyone following us would not be able to see us get into the car. Wow! What kind of a country is this so controlled by the government?

We jumped in the car and were introduced to the very nervous driver who was putting his life at risk by having us in his car. We drove around and around for about twenty minutes to make sure no one was following us, and finally we pulled into the curb of a little row house. David said, "Get out one at a time and go quickly into the house." I did run and soon there we sat with about eight men around a table. All these men were at risk by meeting together in this home with Americans. They even put a pillow over the phone, since the government could listen into conversations without the hook being off.

The government was quite against Christians. For example, one pastor was fined a year's salary for carrying two Bibles in the trunk of his car. A policeman had stopped him and checked his car. One Bible was okay, but two Bibles meant he was proselytizing. The pastor was already poor and had a family of five. All these men were putting themselves at risk to be trained to be leaders of underground churches. Wow! Thank you, Lord, for allowing me to see men who love you so much they are willing to risk losing their jobs, be imprisoned, or losing their financial security, little as it was. Coming from our free country this was so bazaar, but so true.

The teaching began with David and Roger. I was thinking that all this was a bit exciting until a knock came at the door. When I saw the fear on the faces of the men, I knew this was not a fun adventure. My heart started pounding. Was it the secret police? The room became silent, no one moved. Finally, the owner of the house slowly walked to the door as we all sat silently. Phew! The next-door neighbor had just come for cup of sugar. Or was the neighbor curious about finding out why all these people came into their neighbor's home. Would he report it to the police?

Seeing the fright on the men's faces gave me a large clue this was not a safe country to be a citizen let alone a visitor violating state regulations. That occasion gave me a clear picture of the real cost to these Romanian men and women who follow Christ faithfully. One man I talked with lost his job and was beaten severely because he talked to a communist friend about Christ.

Let's go back to the Securitate man at the front door of the hotel. Yes, he was the man who followed us around Romania. When we were finally getting on the bus to the airport the last man on the bus was our man. When I got to the airport and all the suitcases were lined up by the bus, he pointed to my suitcase for me to pick up. How did he know that was my suitcase? He was probably the one who stole my diamond ring I hid in my suitcase in the hotel room.

I was never so happy to get on the plane to fly away from Romania and its dark atheistic government. But, I was privilege to see God along the way in those wonderful, faithful Christian men and women who could not fly away to a free country.

Return to the battle again, no longer trusting in the false and insufficient human resources which so foolishly we had taken into the battle, but now trusting in the limitless resource of our risen Lord. Alan Redpath

YOUR STORY

_____
_____
_____
_____
_____

Chapter 3

AN EXCITING OPPORTUNITY

We were off to Africa on a fact-finding trip for our mission agency, Entrust. We already had our Sunday School Class pray for us and were ready and eager to go. What a privilege to see and report on what God was doing in countries of Africa, "growing leaders for growing churches."

Two days before our departure a friend called and asked if she and her husband could come over to say goodbye. "Sure, come on! Love to have y'all." Why'd they want to see us, I wondered. "Roger, we're about to have guests stop by," I yelled up the stairwell.

When they arrived, we all got comfortable in the living room. Fortunately, I had just made some coffee and cookies moments before they arrived, and we were eager and curious to hear what they had on their minds.

Bob, while munching on a warm chocolate chip cookie said, rather formally, "LJ and I want to give you $1000 so you can donate it to a worthy cause that you might discover in Africa."

Wow! What an exciting opportunity to find a person or ministry with needs that we might be able to help. What a privilege to be able to pass on such a generous gift. We thanked Bob and LJ profusely, prayed and hugged--after we ate all the cookies, of course.

Two hectic days we were packed. Off we went to Africa with the $1000 tucked away in my secret, hidden belt. (Or was it my bra? Oh, well.) But now we had to be really on the alert for that perfect opportunity, just the right project. We wanted it to be someone or some ministry that would reproduce itself in a significant way or have long term effect, not just sandwiches for a picnic.

After a long, exhausting trip, we arrived in Africa. Every part of my body ached. Our itinerary was to visit four countries, Kenya, Mozambique, Uganda and South Africa to evaluate Entrust's ministry there and to see our staff who were strategically working in these countries.

Outside Nairobi we visited Kibera, a shanty town where a million people live in extreme poverty. It was a community where all the houses, (*shacks* would be a better word,) were made of cardboard, or pieces of wood and only a few had tin roofs. There was no in-door plumbing or electricity. "Oh Lord, why are *we* so blessed?" Each shanty was the size of one of our garden sheds, but theirs housed families of eight. So much need. Nothing that a mere thousand dollars could fix.

We visited an orphanage that cared for about 200 children. Next to it was a home for widows. The women wove straw baskets, so they could buy a scraggly chicken for food. The smiling children were dressed in well-worn uniforms. We met the head mistress of the school, a dynamic African woman dressed in a colorful wrap around sarong. She had the children sing for us. They melted our hearts. We knew the tune, *Jesus Loves Me*, but not the words in their language. In a conversation with the head mistress, Mrs. Grace Jusu, she mentioned the village was in great need for another well.

A well! Now that was something that would have continued benefit, but, alas, probably would cost hundreds of dollars. Later that morning, I casually asked, "Mama Grace, how much do you need for the well?" "We need about $200.00 more." Two hundred dollars! "Lord, is this something we should give some of our thousand dollars to?"

After I talked to God and talked it over with Roger, it was decided. We quickly took Miss Grace aside and said that we would like to give the last $200 for the well. She happily wept and hugged us. I could hardly wait to tell Bob and LJ. They would be thrilled to know they had a part in helping that orphanage.

Two hundred well spent dollars--with $800 to go! What a joy it was for us to have carried that gift that would provide fresh water for all those people.

As we continued our trip, it was now hotter, and I was wilting, but we kept looking for another place for another project. Looking for a brief respite, our guide dragged our weather-weary bodies to a fresh vegetable and fruit market that was under some brightly colored canopies. The African man who greeted us asked us where we were from. He mentioned that he had studied Third World Micro-Enterprise in the United States a few years ago. When we asked about his market, he told us how he got a group Christian friends to collect all the scraps of food that were left on the floor of the market each night. They made a compost pile of the food scraps in a back corner of the market. Then they added cow manure to the compost pile and let it dry in the sun for a few days. They had made a small homemade rotating barrel-like sieve with a handle that men and women would take turns operating. They packed the rich compost into heavy paper bags and sold them to be used by the villagers for fertilizing their gardens.

He had formed a co-op with several other Christians to run this little business. They had two cows that happily, each day, donated their manure. They showed us some pictures of the healthy, tall corn that resulted from the use of their *special soil enrichment* and pictures of the fields without the compost supplement. The difference in the growth of the corn was amazing.

Mr. Tshombe and his friends in the co-op now had extra income just from the free vegetable scraps found on the floor of the market. We were impressed with their ingenuity.

Then this weathered and gregarious man with a large smile, told us of a new plan, his dream. He was going to have his workers take the leftover, over ripe, unsold vegetables and fruits from the tables after closing hours, dry them and make them into nutritional supplements for the local children who were often undernourished.

All they needed was money for equipment. The man, "Call me Tschombe" was not giving a pitch for money. He was just telling us what his hoped-for plans were. Yes! A thought. Let's give the money for the needed equipment.

We prayed and then approached Mr. Tschombe as he was leaving. I asked him, "What do you guess your new machine would cost?" "About $750.00." Roger and I gave each other an all-knowing look and then said, "God has led us to give you this gift for your new machine." He was thrilled by the unexpected answer to his prayers, and the help it would bring for the under-nourished children and his little co-op. His huge, pearly white smile said it all.

Because we wanted to be sure that Tshombe knew that the gift we were giving him was from a couple from the States, we told him their names. We gave him their address and said, "Please write a thank you note." He promised he would. And he did.

Truly, a mission Accomplished!

Give generously to your needy brother and do so without a grudging heart; then because of this the Lord your God will bless you in all your work and in everything you put your hand to. There will always be poor people in the land. Therefore, I command you to be openhanded toward your brothers and toward the poor and needy in your land."

Deuteronomy 15: 10-11

YOUR STORY OF AN EXCITING OPPORTUNITY GOD GAVE YOU.

_____
_____
_____
_____
_____
_____

Chapter 4

A NEW SMILE

I love to sing and in the past I was a pretty good soprano. In churches where Roger, my husband, was pastor, I always joined the choir. It's amazing what I could observe while sitting in the choir looking out over the congregation and being distracted from worship by some lady's strange hat or that guys tie that didn't match his rumpled suit.

One Sunday, I peered out at a young couple whom I had not seen before. I determined I would make our congregation one of those "friendly" places. (How many times have you heard the lament that someone had gone to church for five years and no one ever said a welcoming *hello*?)

The first week I saw them I could not get out of the choir loft fast enough to try to make sure they felt welcomed. Several Sundays passed and I never got to connect with the handsome, young couple.

I kept up my weekly frustrated pursuit until one Sunday the young woman was alone. I sensed she looked troubled. The following Sunday she was alone again. *Oh, probably Mr. Whatshisname was working.*

That time, after our final choral ahh-aaa-men, I dashed to intercept this attractive young girl. She was very friendly and animated. Her name was Marie. She gave me a brief summery to my questions that included that she worked in cosmetics at the mall in one of the department stores. She said that she would be pleased to meet me for lunch. "I can meet you during my lunch break--just to talk--and I'm buying," she quickly assured me.

"I'd be honored. Twelve noon, Monday. Thanks very much." I asked God to help me. She seemed troubled. My sixth senses were in full gear. Monday. Twelve sharp.

On Monday we went to a busy lunchroom at the mall. I read the menu and sipped at ice water, then I said: "Tell me about yourself." After a few paragraphs of rapid-fire talking she took a deep breath and, as though in a confessional, her words tumbled out. "I've been searching for God all my life, and I can't seem to find Him!"

The waitress interrupted to take our orders.

"I talked to the chaplain when at college, but He didn't seem to know what I could do to connect with God. Since you're a minister's wife, I just thought that...."

I hadn't expected such a gush of pent-up concern. But I know God arranges those times. I told her of Christ's love for her and how He made a wonderful way for her to come to Him at great cost to Himself. I explained what Christ had done on the cross in order for her to live eternally with Him.

"You can ask Christ to be your Savior?" She said, "Oh yes! I have been searching for him all my life." In the jammed lunchroom we briefly prayed together. She expressed such joy. She seemed to be aglow. But, alas, she had to go back to her job at the cosmetic counter. *"This is a lovely shade of lipstick." "This cream will rejuvenate your sadly, aging face."* But her own face couldn't stop smiling.

"Would you like to meet to study the Bible to discover how you can continue to grow as a Christian?" "Yes." She would check with her boss to see if she could get off for a couple of hours on

Wednesday. I drove home smiling about seeing God along the way. When I arrived home, my new friend had already called and said, "Yes," she could meet on Wednesday. Wow! That was a clear indicator that she was serious about her new step of faith. Nothing brings me more joy then that!

Sunday: it turned out that Marie and her husband were struggling with their marriage. I had read her face accurately. But she had not mentioned it when we were at lunch.

Not much later, after we had been together with the couple, and we had done some marital counseling, she and her husband joined a couples' Bible Study. After about a year my new friend and her husband sadly moved away. Obviously, God had brought her to our town and church, so they could meet her Lord.

What in life could be better than that!

"He is no fool who gives what he cannot keep gaining what he cannot lose." Jim Elliot

YOUR STORY

_____
_____
_____
_____

Chapter 5

AN INCREDIBLE SURPRISE

For five years I worked as a volunteer for *Habitat for Humanity*. Habitat is an organization that uses volunteers to build houses for under privileged people. I liked the challenging experience and worked hard at my assignments. After a couple years I was asked to be the head of the *Nurture and Selection Committee*. That pleased me because it fit some of my spiritual gifts. It was also an honor and I remember I walked taller that week. I was tasked to choose which families would be approved for a Habitat home and helped families adjust after they moved into their new homes. As the houses were being built, it was exciting to see whole families work with the volunteers and to watch relationships develop between volunteers and new residents.

Finally, the first family moved into their perfect, clean, well built, beautiful home -- which even had a bedroom for each child. There were ecstatic screams and yelps of delight -- from everyone, including me. There certainly was no better feeling than to be part of something like that.

After the families were settled in for a few weeks, I would visit them and from time to time inquire if there were questions, concerns, or issues. All usually went well. That was until the second month when, Adam, a single father with three small children, didn't pay his very low monthly rent.

I thought to myself, "He just must have forgotten. All the business of moving and getting kids settled in a new school etc., etc...." So, I made a friendly visit to say "Hi", and casually mentioned that his rent payment was due. He smiled and said, "Oh, I will get right at it. I didn't realize it was time to pay again already. Time's just flying by, Miss Joy." I smiled, and we talked about happy things, the weather, his job, and the neighbors.

Next month...again no payment. When the Habitat Board met I reluctantly reported the issue about Adam not paying. Our inexperienced board passed it off as *forgetfulness*. "It often happens that way due to the adjustments." But I wasn't sure. Next month, no payment! I reported to the Board, "If we let this go on we will just be enabling Adam." They voted to give him another chance. *Hmm.*

Six months later Adam still hadn't paid a cent. (I wanted to report: "I told you so," but thought that might not be a very Christlike act.) Finally, the board moved that I inform and warn Adam that he would have to move out of his home if he remained in arrears. We were all so sad, especially since we all liked him--not only that, but his children would bear the brunt of his irresponsible behavior. But he had to go.

Afterward we learned that he had been involved with drugs and alcohol addictions. How did we let him get a house? We thought we had been very thorough in our background checks. No negative reports or behavior had showed up. But we knew we were doing the right thing in evicting him. There was deep sadness. Tough love is not easy.

Five years later I was in a *Big Lots* store looking for my latest *irresistible deal*. As I was walking down what looked like a promising bargain aisle I heard someone shout, "Mrs. Gulick, how are you?" I turned, and there stood Adam. "Well, I'm fine, but, how are you?" I asked. We hugged. And he said, genuinely beaming, "I'm doing really great! Really great."

I asked with some skepticism, remembering his history, "Are you *really* great, Adam?" He couldn't talk fast enough; he was practically bubbling, "Thank you, thank you for kicking me out of that Habitat house. That brought me to the end of myself. I was, for a while deeply depressed. What had I done to myself and my kids? Later, someone, a good friend, suggested I go with him to his church. I went and soon became a Christian. I have a job and am now buying my own house. Not only that, most importantly I'm off drugs and alcohol."

At this we hugged again and laughed and said how incredible God was. What delight I felt that day when I met Ivory again. The reborn, new Adam! Again, God met me along the way, even in *Big Lots*.

With God all things are possible. Mark 10:27

YOUR STORY OF GOD SURPRISING YOU

_____
_____
_____
_____
_____
_____
_____

Chapter 6

DOUGLAS NORMAN

My family and my extended family, which at last count was about fifty-seven people, fifty-seven relatives that managed to see each other quite a bit. All were Christians trying to follow Christ. Then in the middle of this tribe, a nephew, Doug, got caught up in the 60's culture- you remember- psychedelic drugs, long hair, bell bottom jeans and lots of guitar playing.

One day Doug's "friends" dropped him off at home while he was in the middle of a bad drug trip. My sister, Doug's mother, was aghast and scared, and sadly for the first time acknowledged he was in trouble. She immediately called my counselor brother, Paul, to come and help. Of course, this news swept through our family of Christians like wild fire in a dry forest and prayers started to go up for Doug.

Jump ahead a month. While sitting in my parent's restaurant, my husband and I had a chance to talk with our handsome, blond, hippie nephew. Actually, he was a really great kid. We asked him if he believed there was a God. He said, "I don't know." We then asked, "If there were a God would you want to believe in Him." "Yes," he said, "of course." We then asked him if he would be willing to enter into a thirty-day prayer covenant asking God, "If you are real, reveal yourself to me." He said he would.

Roger and I then began asking every Christian group we had contact with, and we had lots of contacts being pastor and wife, to pray. We asked small groups, churches, friends, conferences and personal contacts. We would get everyone we could to pray for Doug. "The prayers of righteous men availeth much." Every time I woke up in the middle of the night, Doug would come to my mind and I would pray for Him.

Thirty days were up, and we were anxious to see what happened. Doug told us, "Yes, I prayed for 30 days (amazing in itself)." On the 30th day Doug was laying in the sun and he was thinking Christianity must be true, and as he thought that a warm feeling flooded through him. Doug wrote this in a letter to us. "I'm going to enclose a poem I wrote for you and Roger. It's a kind a of thank you note. In other words, God came alive through his Son. Wow! I mean what a realization. When I first understood, I spent awhile away from everybody trying to talk myself out of it. I felt foolish at being happy, but finally I let it flow. I found Christianity wasn't a bind after all and that I could be cool. I mean by giving up my life to God I gained it back again in better shape than it had ever been. Strange things began to happen like unlikely coincidences etc. One day I gave my one valuable possession to a friend, my guitar. He was happy and somehow so was I. It didn't make sense to me, but it worked. I began to become contagious. The more I became loving and understanding the more others responded to me. The beautiful part is that I always had someone to turn to. All the deep questions I asked were answered. I lack one thing though and that is fellowship. My friends at school all began to open their hearts to me and I didn't know what to do. I told them about my experience and asked if they wanted to do some Bible study, but they didn't. Maybe I wasn't sure enough of what I was doing or believing. At these times I went home to church and got myself straight.

Here is the poem he wrote as a new Christian:

I SAW GOD ALONG THE WAY

You

new.

now I

Know

We

Can

Dig It.

We can love. I love you. You love Me.

We Love Them. We love Him. He Loves Us.

Surprised

By

Joy

We

Climb

Higher

To

Meet

Christ

The

Tiger

Forever…

Hallelujah!

We wanted to encourage Doug in his new walk of faith, so we said, "Hey, Doug, why don't you come live with us this summer. We have a job you can do, and you can help us with the youth group." Our college group was the most joyous, spiritual, fun group of college kids we've ever worked with. Doug came and grew spiritually by leaps and bounds and played his guitar for Christ. We also took him to a Young Life leadership camp in Lake Saranac where he got some great biblical teaching. Dr. R.C. Sproul and other teachers were there. He also got to experience incredible fellowship.

Doug just turned sixty-five and retired. Over all these years he has faithfully followed and served Christ with his life and his amazing guitar playing.

Prayer is a strong wall and fortress of the church. It is a godly Christian weapon.

Martin Luther

YOUR STORY -
___
___
___
___
___

Chapter 7

IT HAPPENED AT MACDONALD'S

Ah, MacDonald's, "America's wizardry of fast food" now available around the world. That's not a commercial, just the setting for this story.

For our 50thth wedding anniversary our children gave us a cruise from Australia to New Zealand. We were joyously overwhelmed. While there and sightseeing one pleasantly warm and balmy afternoon - those Aussies do weather very well - we passed a MacDonald's. I know one should never dine at an American fast food place when visiting an exotic place, but we were on a budget. As I was saying, it was a beautiful day and there were MacDonald's Golden Arches - tables outside surrounded by a lovely little park. It was all just for us.

As we were eating our Quarter Pounders, an attractive, young, Asian woman sat down at the next table. Being friendly, I came up with a non-creative greeting, "Isn't this a beautiful day?" That got the conversation going. As we began chatting, she said her name was Mila. (I wiped a bit of ketchup from my chin.) and that she was a Uyghur, a Muslim group from Western China. She began a biography about how she had been living on a yacht for the last seven years with a very wealthy man she met while studying English at Beijing

University. They had spent much of their time sailing to every port in the Far East. Whenever they were not on the yacht, they would stay at five-star hotels and eat at five-star restaurants. She told us, "I would lie on the deck of the yacht, be served fantastic meals and just read book after book." (I was ready for that.)

In retrospect, I am not sure what made her so open with us. She shared that after seven years of her idyllic life, it all became very empty. She was now twenty-eight and wanted to be married and have children, but her Mr. Wonderful was not interested in that. So, she left him. She then told us, through tears, how lonely she was. Yes, she dated some, but she was so used to the rich life and the men she met didn't have much money.

Finally, Roger said, "Joy and I are followers of Christ, and it is our custom to pray about difficult situations people are going through. Would it be alright if I prayed for you?" "I'm Muslim. But, yes, please do." Roger thanked God for loving her and wanting her to experience his love and guidance. He prayed that she would know God's love and guidance for her future.

We talked on and on and finally she thanked us for our prayer and gave us her business card and said good bye. We told her that if she ever came to the States to please come and visit us.

The next day, Sunday, Roger and I attended the Sydney Anglican Cathedral. It was a very alive and vibrant worship service. During the coffee time after worship we met one of the pastors. We shared with him the story of Mila and asked if he would contact her. We gave him her card and he noticed that her apartment was a block from the cathedral. He said he would call her.

Several days later we called the pastor to enquire if there had been any contact. "Yes, I called her the next day and asked to meet her for tea." When they met, she told him things weren't that bad. "I guess I'd just gotten a bit emotional during that conversation." The pastor thought it was all over, but the next day she called him back. "I didn't tell you the truth." She then admitted that she was very lonely and hurting. He invited her to his home for dinner to meet his wife and another Christian couple. Later that week Mila attended a Wednesday evening healing service. We haven't heard the final story yet, but still pray for her and believe that day in Sydney, God had met us and her along the way.

"We live by faith and not by sight" 2 Corinthians 5:7

YOUR STORY ABOUT AN UNEXPECTED MEETING:

_____
_____
_____
_____
_____
_____

Chapter 8

WE'RE RUNNING OUT OF MONEY

My new husband, Roger, had just completed three years at sea as a naval officer. His plan was to attend seminary in beautiful, warm Southern California. We could hardly wait. The pictures I had in my mind of California were blue skies, beautiful beaches and lush foliage. However, when we arrived on campus there was a smog alert, 104-degree temperatures that soon rose to 114. For several weeks we did not know that the San Gabriel mountains were just north of our apartment until one day it rained. The thick, choking, smog cleared away. Behold, there were the magnificent, awesome mountains.

After we settled in, I began looking for a teaching job. Our financial status was quite crimped. But, not to worry, Roger, a math major in college, was a whiz at calculating finances. After his first semester while he was studying Greek, he announced: "Joy, I've got to tell you something. So, please sit down." There was a long pause. Then, awkwardly, "At the rate it is going now, we will run out of money before I finish school." I didn't even blink. "Roger, dear, I have some news, too. (long pause.) I'm pregnant. So why don't we have some ice cream."

My announcement and the ensuing celebration meant: "No more going out to eat—except, well maybe just once a week at our low budget, favorite, cheap Chinese restaurant, ($1.10 for soup, entrée and a fortune cookie). Hey, we were young, and life was good. God would help us work it out. And we were in California!

Poor Roger. He not only was studying, but to help with finances he began cleaning doctors' offices, working part time with Allied Van Lines and in the summer did yard work. I taught school our first year and was sick many mornings. Each week, like Chicken Little's falling sky, my marvelous, worried, young, exhausted husband announced the doom: "We're running out of money." I suggested we have some more ice cream: strawberry.

I began babysitting for three babies for our neighbor (It was my apprenticeship.) while she taught school. Things were very tight, our finances and my shrinking clothes. A girlfriend, whose husband was also attending seminary, and I visited the Salvation Army discount store to buy barely worn clothes donated for the poor by the grand dames of nearby Beverly Hills. We took our shopping spree treasures home, washed, starched and pressed our finds and proudly wore them without a whisper of where we had purchased them. We were the good wives helping our husbands.

But God came *along the way* with other plans than having us run out of money during the time in seminary. Roger was learning Greek, and homiletics and a deeper spirituality when unbeknownst to him, the Navy surprisingly remembered that they had not paid him for being a naval reservist. So, they sent a big back payment check delivered *special delivery*.

During his senior year Roger and I took on a youth worker's position that also helped a great deal. Though faithful Roger, with his green visor on his forehead, kept calculating and wearyingly announcing that we would soon be broke, not only did we not run out of money during those youthful years, we made it across country to our first church with $500 in the bank.

We still smile about those days.

"Treasure up these words in your heart. Be faithful and diligent in keeping the commandments of God and I will encircle you in the arms of my love."

YOUR STORY OF GOD AND MONEY

_____
_____
_____
_____
_____

Chapter 9

HERE'S TO AUNT HELEN

I have always been a story teller. And I like to make people laugh. Most of my verbal anecdotes are shared at parties or with family members. It's part of my heritage. I fondly remember an aunt who was a fantastic story teller. Aunt Helen, a tiny, wise lady whom the Lord gave five boys, was born in Scotland. Her wonderful brogue unselfconsciously enhances stories about herself and her foibles.

Finally, in her tradition and on impulse, I wrote some stories of what I experienced as a pastor's wife. They included a bit of Aunt Helen's wit that I inherited. Probably because of that, some people encouraged me to put them into a book. I thought about doing that and titling it: <u>The Perfect Pastor's Wife</u>. It has a subtitle: <u>Another Book of Fiction</u>.

But what I didn't suspect was how insecure I was going to feel as I considered sharing my stories and my foibles. "They won't like it." "They'll laugh *at me* instead of *with me*." "What if my friends think the stories are awful?"

Several years later, and with the enthusiastic vigor of someone lost in an unfamiliar wilderness, I published my first book about the trials and frustrations of being the wife of a pastor. Being insecure--no, terrified-- about whether people would want to read the book, or pay for it, I found it hard even to say, "I just published a book."

Unfortunately, a major family trait was that one should never be proud or feel self-important--even the Bible says that. But there was my new, first-time-at-writing book, in all its glory. What was I to do? Could I really ask people to buy it?

I, in a rush of anxiety, decided I could give away all the money I made to a mission organization. But which one? I pulled a blank. A couple days later, no fireworks, no blinding light, the obvious came to mind. Our mission. Give the money I make on my book to *Entrust*. "No, not *my* book." Guilt was my next feeling. But then I figured that that was a great idea. "Yes!" Now, at least that was settled. I could relax. Almost.

Would the book sell? Hopefully. Maybe just a few copies. Then, at least, I won't have to be worried about being rich and famous…at least famous.

Some time later I attended an R.C Sproul conference in Florida. My book had been published and immodestly had a bright hot pink cover. I decided I would take some of those newly minted books to the conference--just in case I ran into some old friends who might not think I was too pushy and kindly wanted to read it. I just needed their first impressions. "Oh, God, protect my fragile ego. Amen." How much better it would be to have some publishing house push the book for me.

At the conference I surprisingly ran into a cousin that I hadn't seen for several years. I thought, "I'll give her a book." At the seminar break I ran to the car to get a couple books, just in case I ran into some other people. When I returned to the meeting I placed the books next to me on the seat at the meeting. After the speaker's talk, for some reason, I said a quick prayer: "Lord, sell my two books.

Please."

Just then a couple behind me leaned over the back of my chair and asked, "Where did you get those books?"

I said, "They're mine".

"Who wrote it?"

"I did," I replied shyly.

"I want to buy them both."

Surprised and amazed, I muttered, *Thank you, Lord. Someone wanted my book! Wow.* The "Literary Digest" would soon be calling. I was beginning to be a tad more secure. *Oh, let the book be an encouragement to them, Lord.*

The next day in a plenary session of about 5000 people, the woman who bought my books took the effort to find me in the crowd and said, "I read your book all last night and laughed and loved it."

God gave me great encouragement that beautiful, sunny morning in Florida. If He wanted to sell my books for me, what better manager could I get?

Oh, *Aunt Helen in heaven, thank you for being such a wonderfully funny, wry lady. Amen.*

"The Lord is my strength and my shield, my heart trusts in Him, and I am helped. My heart leaps for joy and I will give thanks to Him in song." Psalm 28:7.

YOUR STORY OF TAKING A RISK:

_____
_____
_____
_____

Chapter 10

MAXIMO

Our son Tim and his wife, Annette, are missionaries in Buenos Aries, Argentina. Once, we took a cruise with them from Buenos Aires to Santiago, Chile around Cape Horn. We stopped in one port in central Argentina. We had read in a tourist guide about a Scottish village a few miles from that city. Since my mother grew up in Scotland, we all thought it would be fun, maybe, even interesting, to go there, so we hired a taxi for a few hours. We had discovered that was the cheapest way to do short excursions. The driver said his name was Maximo.

The four of us piled into the aged taxi and we were soon in a quaint town that looked like a charming, English village. There was a small church on one corner that appeared as though it had just been transplanted from small town in the Highlands. After an hour of walking around playing tourist, I discovered a quaint tea room. Surprise. Surprise. Not that it mattered, but it was nearly lunchtime (at least somewhere in the world). So, I, as a quorum of one, decided we'd have lunch there.

As typical American tourists, and being ignorant of local customs, we invited Maximo, our cab driver, to join us. He seemed a bit surprised but agreed. "Si, si. Senora." As we sat around the table waiting for our lunches, son, Tim, being his usually creative self, came up with the idea of having each of us describe what we most liked about holidays and how we celebrated them. (Tim and Annette were translating. Soon Maximo got into the fun by telling us what his family did at Christmas and for weddings and birthdays. Though he was living in Argentina, he grew up in Uruguay. We all laughed at how he had to learn different customs when he moved from one country to the next. We laughed even more when he told us how very odd our American customs seemed.

It was a very pleasant and fun time and I felt Maximo really got insight into what our families were like. (One thing, we all talk at once.) As we drove back to where we were to board our ship, Maximo asked through Tim, "What is it that your family has? I have never met any family who relates so well with one another, as I have seen you all do. Whatever you have, I think the whole world's looking for it."

Maximo's wistful question received a warm response from Roger my husband;
"You can have what we have." He began to explain to our new friend that it was our relationship with Jesus Christ that was at the center of each of our lives and our lives together. As Tim kept up a speedy translation, Annette, Tim's wife and I prayed in the back seat of the taxi. There were a number of questions that Maximo asked and finally he said, "I want Christ in my life. What do I have to do?"

Since we needed to return to the ship quickly, Maximo had been driving quite fast as he listened to the Gospel presentation. (I was hoping that he wasn't told to close his eyes and pray). We were almost to the dock when he asked God to forgive his sins and asked Christ to come into his life as his Savior and Lord.

We arrived at the ship, which was about to depart. Tim quickly told Maximo to get a Bible, start reading the Gospel of John and find a church that taught the scriptures.

That was all the time we had. "Everyone, please, please get on board!" Once on the ship we prayed for Maximo, for God to bring a caring person across his path, to continue His work in our new Argentine brother whom we had met along the way.

"Beware in your prayers, above everything else, of limiting God, not only by unbelief, but by fancying that you know what He can do."
Andrew Murray

YOUR STORY

_____
_____
_____
_____
_____

Chapter 11

AN UNEXPECTED HELP

Our daughter, having just graduated from college, was now on her way to the adult life of paying for her apartment, food, gas, clothes, insurance, fun, infinitum. Of course, having graduated from a good college and being bright she would get a job quickly. Wrong! Would you believe part time waitressing at a country club and helping at a coffee shop?

Reality set in after a few months and soon we received a phone call, that her outgo was larger than her income. Her car insurance bill could not be paid. Our family policy was not to rescue too quickly but said we would pray. Pray we did.

One morning on Roger's day off, and thus mine, as we were praying for young wise educated Kathleen to find a job, the phone rang. It was my nephew who worked for a College outside Philadelphia. He was asking if the college's choir could come and sing at our church. Then it popped into my head to ask him if there was any possible, itsy bitsy job our daughter could do at the college. He replied quickly and said, "There might just be one. I'll call you back in about ten minutes." Ten minutes it was.

"They are looking for someone to do student recruitment for the college. Can Kathleen come for an interview in two weeks?" Wow! Lord that was a quick answer. We called Kathleen, and it held some interest to her, but that would mean leaving all her college friends in the area which would not be easy to do. But the timing certainly made her more open to moving. She didn't even have the money to fly for the interview. No problem, the school would reimburse her.

There were two girls applying for the job, and the other girl graduated from the recruiting college, so the chance for Kathleen to get the job was slim. We upped our prayer time and soon we heard those wonderful words. "I got the job!"

We celebrated and marveled at how the very moment we had been praying we had received the phone call.

"Faith expects from God what is beyond expectation." Andrew Murray

YOUR STORY OF WONDERFLLY ANSWERED PRAYER:

_____

_____

_____

_____

_____

Chapter 12

THE EMPTY GAS TANK

After graduating from college, I was asked to join the staff of Young Life, a Christian organization whose primary focus is high school students. I was assigned to Baltimore, Maryland. All staff, like any itinerant missionary, must raise their own salary and living expenses from generous Christian friends. I hadn't raised all the money I needed to live on, but my new boss, Jerry Johnson, graciously said, "Oh, just come on to Baltimore and we'll see what money we can raise here." I eagerly took his suggestion in that I was anxious to begin my work as a newly minted *Billy Graham* in training.

I had no car, only $20.00 in my purse, no apartment, but lots of trust in a caring God. (I envisioned God calling a staff meeting of angels, saying, "We've got a tough new assignment on our hands.") Happily, when I arrived, I was told that one of the other staff girls had an extra room in her apartment. I could live there. So, with my overstuffed and battered suitcase, I moved into her third floor room. The room desperately needed a visit from Martha Stewart, but I was grateful for the space. Thank you, Lord.

Jerry's first generous effort was to help me get some transportation so that I could travel the miles from high school campus to campus, my new mission field. Jerry brought all his clever skills to bear and his knowledge of the city, and together we found an old junker, a stick shift, Bel Aire Chevrolet for about $150.00 dollars. I would eventually pay it off with my gigantic Young Life salary. I came to love and depend on that Ole Lizzy. It got me around and all the kids liked to bounce around in my old, old car. The high schools seemed to all have the latest models.

But the real picture--please laugh with me--was of an earnest, eager, idealistic recent college graduate living on the edge. Once, for instance, at the local gas station I bought 29 cents of gas, which in 1959 was a whole gallon. My new boyfriend, Roger, was a lieutenant in the Navy. He would come to visit me when his ship was in port at the Philadelphia Navy Yard. Every time he came to visit me we'd have a great time, but as we drove around, always at an absolutely inappropriate time, one of my tires would go flat and we'd have to blump, blump to the curb. Ever loving Roger, in order to keep me alive, ended up buying his favorite, struggling missionary new tires, because she was so broke. Embarrassed too.

One night, during my "in training" Baltimore adventure, I was riding alone from the Young Life office on a very busy street to my *deluxe* apartment in my minimally functioning car. Absentmindedly, I glanced at the gas gauge and slowly realized that it showed empty. "Oh, I can make it, it's just a few more miles," I thought, hopefully. But I was wrong! So very wrong. At that moment, the car sputtered and coughed as I pulled over to the side of the road. The engine then gasped and died.

"Oh, Lord, now what!"

In just a moment, a car pulled up behind me. A middle aged, nicely dressed man got out of his car and came over to my very slightly opened window.

"Miss, are you O.K.?"

"I've run out of gas." I was terrified. Many headlines soared through my vivid imagination. *Beautiful youth leader abducted! Innocent young woman accosted on lonely highway!*

The stranger very kindly said, "I'll be right back with some gas. I own a gas station."

"Oh, thank you, thank you, I gratefully said. He drove off as I thought about what just had happened. I had just run out of gas and immediately thought, "Why me. Where are you, Lord." I wanted to scream, but instead yelled, "Are you there, Lord?" I was alone, broke and no one cared. But a man stopped behind my disabled car about a second after the Chevy gasped its last breath. And he owned a gas station! Incredible!

In minutes the very nice man (angel?) was back and pouring gas into the thirsty tank. My genuine gratefulness was followed quickly by embarrassment. "Thank you, thank you!" I said profusely, "But I only have sixteen cents in my wallet. Can I get your address and send you what I owe for the gas and your generosity?"

"Oh, Miss, don't worry. I have a daughter your age and I would want someone to help her if she ran out of gas. You don't need to pay me anything. It was my pleasure. Have a nice evening."

Off he went, and I drove off with tears running down each cheek, knowing that God had certainly met me along the way.

Be still and know that I am God. Psalm46:16

YOUR STORY

CHAPTER 13

A CURIOUS HAPPENING

One Tuesday I happened by Roger's church office to accomplish some little task. I sat down at the welcome desk right inside the church's front door. I rarely sat there, but it gave me some space to write. I hadn't been there very long when the phone rang. There were secretaries at the church, but I thought I would save them one more interruption. I picked up the phone on the desk and gave a friendly greeting, "Good morning, First Presbyterian Church!"

"Hello, this is Mrs. Holt and I was wondering if there is anyone in your church who would be willing to take a Russian exchange student into their home. There is a boy, a high school senior, from the Caucuses region of Russia who is on the plane as we speak. The family here who was going to take this exchange student into their home for a year just cancelled out."

"Oh, my," I said. "How awful!" She continued with a desperate voice and said, "If we could just find someone to take him for two weeks until we can get someone long term it would be wonderful." I thought to myself that I could take someone for two weeks. In my mind I thought this could be a great way to evangelize in a caring, non-invasive way. I could do anything for two weeks. I mentioned to her that I was having a Mexican girl come to stay for six months, so it could only be two weeks at our house. She assured me, it would only be two weeks." Okay then, when he arrives bring him to our home." I gave her all the details of where we lived and went home to clean. A lick and a promise was an expression my mother always used for a quick house cleaning job. I think I just licked, I didn't have time for the promise.

I thought to myself, "Strange that I just happened to answer that phone that day."

Eldar, the Russian exchange student, arrived. He was a Muslim and very home sick already. He was a tall good looking young man and seemingly very bright. We found out that next year he would be heading for one of the best universities in Russia, St. Petersburg. We had a large bedroom for him and also a swimming pool in the back yard, so we thought he would have a great time for two weeks.

All was well until it came time for dinners. He would look at my very delicious food and say, "Could you take me to MacDonald's?" I asked him, "Is there something I can make you that you might like?" "Could you take me to MacDonald's," he would say in his broken English? I was puzzled. I would ask, "Do you have some favorite food I could make?" "No," he would say. I began to wonder if there was some Muslim thing that I was violating. "MacDonald's please." So off to MacDonald's we went. Stupid of me, I know, but I wanted him to have a good beginning, and it was only going to be two weeks!

At the end of two weeks, the friendly exchange student coordinator lady called, not to make arrangements to pick up Eldar, but to say, "We haven't found a family yet. Do you know anyone who might want an exchange student?" The handwriting was on the wall. Did God want Eldar in our home?

We took him in, but I kept looking for a good host family. I did finally find a family after two months. Thank you, Lord! One month later the front door bell rang and there stood Eldar and his host mother wearing a frown. She handed him back to me. "He is the most selfish person I have ever met!" Okay, I got it! Eldar was now *our* exchange student.

I could tell you many stories about the year of our Russian exchange student, but the one that made it all worthwhile and where we saw God along the way happened a short time before he left. Eldar would never go to church with us since he was Muslim, although other Muslim students would attend. He wouldn't budge on that subject. Each night and morning when we ate together we would hold hands and give thanks for the meal and for God's faithfulness. We had many talks about what Christianity was about and he did ask lots of questions. He went through our Christian holidays with us and of course we bought him Christmas presents to open on Christmas morning with our family.

We kept praying for Eldar and for a breakthrough. A friend of ours got a copy of the "Jesus" film on DVD in Eldar's language, Balkar. The likelihood of him watching the "Jesus" film was minimal. I kept praying about how we could get him to watch it. The thought came to me (I believe a God thought.) "Eldar, why don't you watch this film? It will give you an understanding of the meaning of the stories depicted in the church windows in St. Petersburg." Since he was very bright and very much into learning, He agreed.

We all went upstairs and watched the entire film of the life of Christ…in Balkar. We listened like it was our own language afraid to move lest we cause him to get up and leave. Generally, Eldar would walk out in the middle of most wholesome Hollywood movies, but not this time. At the end of the film, we could tell that an invitation to receive Christ was given and Eldar never flinched. He said the actors spoke his language like a native, but he said there were no Christians in Balkar. We said apparently there were some. He couldn't believe it. He had never run into a Christian there.

A few weeks, it was time for Eldar to go home after a year in the states. He left all the gifts of clothing and fun gifts we gave him at Christmas. We have no idea why. But as he was walking out with his duffle bag, we said, "Would you like to take the "Jesus" film? He opened up his bag and took it. We were both astonished and amazed that he did.

That is not the end of the story. With our new task of pastoring missionaries, we had trips to Russia. Guess who one time picked us up at the Airport and took us to dinner and dropped us off at our bed and breakfast. Right, Eldar! We have seen him in Russia two times now and the last time we saw him he said, "I am so glad I was put in your home." He also said that he believes in Jesus as well as Mohammed. We believe God is continuing to work in his life and he continues to ask questions.

Did God have me there to answer the telephone that day in the church? You betcha!

That was not the last time we had contact with Eldar. Four years after he was in our home the thought came that I should reach out and clearly present to him the good news of Christ. I was a bit hesitant, but I knew God was prompting me to do this. So, I wrote him the following letter. His amazing response follows.

Dear Eldar,

How are you? Anything new in your life? Still going with the same girl friend or have you broken up? How's work? We still have great memories of our time together in Moscow. You were so kind to us and even though it was cold, we really enjoyed ourselves. Actually, it was kind of fun to have the cold snow hit our faces.

I am writing because as I was having coffee at Starbucks today, I got thinking about you. I realized that we care a lot about you and I really never shared the most important thing in my life, Christ. We talked a little about it, but not very much. I know your Koran says to listen to Christ's book. The wonderful thing about what the Bible says is "God so loved the world that he gave his only Son (Christ), that whoever believes in Him would not perish, but have eternal life. (John 3:16). I want you to know Christ and how much He loves you and wants you to be one of His children, so you can have eternal life. Eternal life cannot be earned by our good works, because we always fall short of God's standard. It is a free gift since Christ paid the penalty for our sins by taking them on himself and dying on the cross. And we know it is true because He was resurrected on the third day after being buried. When we pray and ask Christ into our lives, he sends His Holy Spirit into our lives and gives us a new desire to please Him and live for Him. Christ already loves you and desires you to come to him and live for him and experience the joy and peace he gives. If you want to know more about this, get a Bible and read the book of John. This is a good place to start reading about who Christ is and what life is all about.

I hope this doesn't turn you off or hurt our friendship, but I would hate for you to miss out on the incredible life Jesus offers.

We are going to Austria in April. I'm in charge of a Women's Conference for about fifty people. Did we tell you we went with Tim and Annette to Argentina in February? They have moved there now to do work with youth leaders. That was a great time. We helped paint their apartment and helped them get settled in their new country.

We then went to Disney World with Kathleen and Dan and the two boys during spring break. We all loved it. Watching the boys made it even more fun.

The weather here is very erratic. One day it is 70 degrees and the next day it is snowing. I can't wait till spring is here. I know Moscow will be wonderful in the spring and summer.

Write and tell us about yourself. Do you have any new possibilities about coming to the states? Our doors are always open.

Warmly,

Joy Gulick

HELLO JOY!!

It is a great pleasure to hear from you! I really like when people write letters to others right after they have had thoughts, when they share things that they have on their minds!

I am still dating the same girl, so I am stable here, but we are on the same positions in our relationship so maybe I am too stable. Work is good; P&G is having double digit growth on Russian market, so I am having enough of it.

Your words about Christ surely will never hurt our friendship and will not turn me off, I see it as a real honor to me that you're caring about people that are close to you, and I think I am close to you somehow. I do love Christ just as all other prophets and I do know a lot how he suffered for all of us and that he took the pain of all people. I totally agree with you on everything that you've written, that faith must dominate in souls of all humans and I am trying to be more spiritual in right kind of way and I am 100% positive that both Islam and Christianity are absolutely common on this issue as well as Judaism because we all have the same roots!

Wow, you've been to Argentina and Disney! Happy for you! You are real road warriors! I am glad that all your family is doing great! You don't have spring yet? We DO have it in Moscow! 60 Fahrenheit! I am planning my vacation in June but I have not decided where to go yet, but if I am to visit US you surely will see me, and I will see you! We will have a new president as of May, what do you think of him?

All the best that WORLD can give.

Eldar

Our story with Eldar is not over. We are still praying.

YOUR STORY OF THE SURPRISING THINGS GOD DOES:

_____
_____
_____
_____
_____
_____

Chapter 14

TENNIS ANYONE?

Roger was diligently working on his doctorate at a southern California seminary. He had to go there at least twice a year. I was raising two kids. (Well that's special too.)

Needing a break from his intense study of "Pastoral Counseling" and "Equipping the Saints for Ministry" one Saturday afternoon Roger made an easy decision to take a break and play some tennis in the city courts. (*I'll get back to studying in....well...only an hour, he told himself.*) The public courts were unusually busy that afternoon, so the procedure was that when a court was open the next four players in line would get to play doubles. (There was no one-on-one luxury.) So, Roger teamed up with three guys he had never met before. It turned out to be a great match and Roger felt he had never played better. After the set, his partner, a guy, Hollis Chang, invited Roger to play on his court back at his home. Of course, regardless of having to study "Equipping the Saints" or "Pastoral Counseling" for that matter, Roger said a hearty *yes*. Little did he suspect that God had a different task for him that afternoon.

When they arrived, Hollis' wife, Linda, and her friend, Lee Ming, had just completed a set on their court and suggested a foursome. "But let me make some iced tea first." (Ah, the California life style. And don't forget, I'm back home changing diapers!)

"The chilled drinks were minted and refreshing". Linda, Hollis casually said, "You'll get a kick out of this. Roger is a Presbyterian minister."

"Welcome to our home," she bowed slightly. "So, you are a minister. Is it true you have to be born again to be a Christian?"

"Yes."

That was exactly the way the conversation began. This was going to be an interesting afternoon. Off the four went to play a brisk set of tennis on an exquisite court. The players were well matched and played a vigorous game. After the game, Linda graciously said to Roger, "We'd be very honored to have you stay for dinner." She bowed slightly.

"Well, I really should be studying, but...well, yes, I'd love too." Roger and Hollis took quick showers in the backyard cabana. After a delightful dinner which continued into the dusk, the doctor excused himself saying that he had to be at the hospital by 5:30 and desperately needed some sleep. Lee Ming also had an early call and said that she too needed to get home.

In the designer appointed kitchen Roger and Linda began to discuss Linda's earlier question. They were the simple questions that so many seekers have about what it means to become a Christian. She had been involved in a neighborhood Bible study and was just learning that trying to be a nice person was not what it meant to become a follower of Christ and a child of God. Obviously, this was a divine appointment because that night God added one more to his family when Cho solemnly said that this faith was what she had been looking fo,for years. Roger prayed for her and then said his good night.

A few days later, Linda, our new Christian sister asked Roger if he would please baptize her and her children. Roger was thrilled and made the arrangements.

Linda and Hollis invited both Roger and me to stay in their guest house behind their pool which was behind their tennis court which was behind their lovely Spanish architecture home whenever Roger had to be at his California seminary to study. This was so wonderful because that gave Roger (and me, when I could go with him) more time to develop our friendship with them and help them become established in a church.

It turned out that a casual meeting on a tennis court was God's way of transforming for eternity a whole family. (Oh...yes, I discovered Hollis was the son of a pastor who had left the ministry. He too had dropped out of involvement in the things of Christ. But this divine appointment on the tennis court made a big difference in his life too.)

He who kneels before God can stand before anyone.

YOUR STORY

_____

_____

_____

_____

_____

_____

Chapter 15

THE GREEN MAMBA

It was two years after my young conversion at our local Baptist church that a missionary was invited to speak. I was sixteen. The missionary graphically spoke of the savage Auca Indians in Ecuador and the heroic missionaries who were speared to death while trying to bring them the good news of Christ. At the end of his talk the pastor challenged anyone to stand if they were willing to be a missionary. Scary stuff, I thought. But my heart was moved, so I stood: "Yes, I was willing."

Of course, in my young, naive teens I had counted the cost of losing my life, or at least, living in a difficult, threatening jungle amongst the naked savages. I had no idea what I was committing to. Soon after that transfixing event I was off to college to PREPARE FOR THE MISSION FIELDS OF DARKEST AFRICA, or maybe just southern Paris or Hawaii would do? (May we have a trumpet fanfare, please.) Not surprisingly, God had a different plan for me. I remember the plaque I once saw that said, "If you want to give God a chuckle, just tell him your plans," I was to be the wife of a minister! (Over the years I discovered that being a pastor's wife frequently meant there would be times when I *might* lose my life or be humiliated by the local savages. But more of that later. But back then, somewhere in the Dark Ages, I think, back when I was sixteen, God had started a clever testing process to see if I were willing to go anywhere He sent me. It was called marriage, mother and pastor's wife.

Move ahead thirty-five years. Pastor/husband Roger was now senior minister of a congregation much involved in world missions. I was fifty. We had two grown children in college and a mortgage. A visiting missionary that our church supported asked Roger and me if we would like to go with him for a couple weeks to Liberia, Africa. We would teach and speak at the *African Bible College's* graduation. Wow! That sounded exciting. (And possibly no naked savages), this was a Bible college. A short time later another missionary asked us to go to Romania to do some teaching as well. Hmm, what was God up to? Africa? Communist countries? Muslims? Was this the moment to pick up from where I, a sixteen-year-old urchin, who was afraid, but valiant, had left off?

Soon, tickets were bought, bags were packed, passports were in order, and I discovered how far away Africa was from our little, tidy, safe home. The flight from South Carolina to Africa took forever. Every cell in my aging body ached from the twenty plus hours I sat in one of those tiny (coach fare) seats. At the very end of my tether and tolerance we finally landed in Monrovia, Liberia in West Africa. There had been no non-stop plane from South Carolina. So it was a multi change plane trip. (It turned out Monrovia was not anyone's favorite vacation spot.) Roger and I got off, I hoped, the last plane-- which minutes before had bumped down a dirt runway toward a little wooden shack at one end. That turned out to be the *luxury passenger area*. The missionary traveling with us said in a matter of fact way, "Do *not* give your suitcase to any of the men who offer to carry it for you. They *will* carry it to the terminal and then demand that you pay them to get it back." No problem, I could carry my rather heavy suitcase. (Why hadn't they invented wheeled suitcases by then?) I was strong and willful. Just watch.

Wrong! As I got off the plane, four scruffy looking, young men, grabbed for my suitcase. But I held tight. Didn't matter. In a flash it was out of my tired hands. Yes, I paid money to the competing young men to get it back. In the meantime, strong, manly Roger, who hates paying tips, didn't fare any better. Round one: AFRICA. Portents of things to come?

Bedraggled and defeated we finally boarded a rickety van that took us to the *African Bible College* (ABC) in Yekepa, two hours north of Monrovia. There was only a dirt road, green jungle, (*heart of darkest Africa*), monkeys-screaming welcomes all along the way. It was beautiful, awesome, scary and forever. We traveled those bumpy, dusty roads - a National Geographic prize photo - for unending hours.

I nearly dosed off on our bumpy ride when two imposing soldiers with automatic weapons were holding a rope across the dirt road. Our host whispered, "Say nothing." That part was easy. But my stomach began to complain. Who were these seemingly angry, very black, scary looking guys? It turned out they were the Liberian version of a military check point. Yet were they there to capture or kill us? Not us nice missionaries. Yet, we were subjected to two more of those harmless, but potentially deadly check points on the way. All my fearful, childhood fantasies were in full flower. You want "heart of darkest Africa? You've got it."

The ride, with all its anxieties, was long, hot and unsettling. We were exhausted from our very long air odyssey. I was looking forward to hearing, "May I serve you a cool drink, a cool cloth to refresh your face?" As any good *American Express* travel adventure boastfully proclaims: *You will finally arrive at a awesome, lush green campus with swaying palm trees, manicured lawns and Home and Garden landscaping with every tropical flower and frangipani that God created exclusively for Eden and you.* That was not quite what we found: the buildings were simple, inelegant, and well kept. The compound consisted of a college with over 200 Africans students studying Christian Leadership. Exciting! A jungle oasis. In case we were too much under the spell of Alice's Wonderland, as we got out of the van and gazed at this new paradise, one of the young missionaries warmly welcomed us (it was also a staggering, humid 100 degrees in the shade) and said off hand-idly, "Oh, by the way, you'll need to stay alert while you're here. This time of the year there are many green mambas. One killed our German Shepherd last week."

"Green what?"

"Mambas. They're big, green snakes that can kill a dog in 30 minutes and us in an hour."

Oh, great! Just like I knew it would be in my wildest teenage imaginings. My mind said: Joy, grow up. He's only kidding. My body went into alert mode. Here we go... It was going to be *dying for Christ*.

Yes, of course, he wasn't kidding; there *were* green mambas, but that wasn't all. All the bugs native to the Carolinas were there, plus many more, and all three or four times the size of our cute little domestic critters. African moths looked like attack birds. Rhinoceros beetles were at least three inches long. Small lizards crawled over all the walls. At least *they* wouldn't kill us. *Would they?*

By contrast, and after I took a deep breath and looked around more carefully, I saw that everything in the campus was neat and clean. And all the buildings were white and lovely. The students were very welcoming. We felt very comfortable. I was so exhausted that night that I slept better than when under any surgical gas in the hospital.

The next morning, whatever was in the local water, my hair could do no wrong. It was full and soft and practically arranged itself in a style I had always tried to explain to my hairdresser. Next day, all refreshed, Roger and I taught some classes. What a team. We are not quite sure how culturally relevant we were, and I still cringe to think about how off the mark we probably were, ugh. Live and learn! The second evening we were invited to dinner with the education staff. We had a great time getting to know each other and talking and laughing. (I'm always good if I get to laugh.) It was 9:00 when it was time for us still-jet-lagged-people to go to our rooms. Oh, thank you Lord.

Remembering the green mambas, I very nicely, very casually asked, "Oh, would it be possible for someone to drive us home, please?" Home was just several hundred feet across their back yard. But I was certain that behind that house were miles of tall grasses shrouded in darkness--the perfect place for the green mambas that would bite...and kill, and many other dangerous critters, and all that stuff that goes "bump" in the night. Our hostess laughed and said, "Don't worry, Joy, just stamp your feet really hard and you'll scare them away." Yea, right! But I knew they were serious. That increasingly familiar knot gripped my stomach again as I just thought about that *very short walk* in the dark, to the safety of our cottage. (Had Roger remembered to bring the Maalox?) *I couldn't believe they were already sending us out to be killed by the Mambas.* But we heroically went out and obeyed their suggestion and stamped our feet as we walked. (Onward, Christian, Stamping Soldiers.) We made it safely to the guest house, but not without a few more gray hairs. So much for faith! (There was a rumor among the students the next morning that there had been a small earthquake the evening before at about 9:00. How come I missed that?

Come morning I looked out at the front porch. And, of course, there was a beautiful, green, four-foot-long Mamba curled up contentedly just outside our door. Did you hear me!?... Outside our door! The snake was even *leaning* against the door! Just think, we could have easily opened that front door just for a refreshing breath of tropical morning air and walked out only to be bitten by that scary, lethal green snake. We'd be dead in an hour. I knew it, I just knew it. (Do you sense my calm, cool demeanor?) But God had other plans for us that day.

Did I tell you about the spitting cobras; they live in that area, too, and can spit twenty feet or more and their venom blinds a person? But the school property lawn was mowed, so I didn't think they could hide in the grass and get me. Slowly I began to calm down and put the spitting cobras out of my mind. (Well, sort of). And, of course I prayed for a sense of peace.

Several days later Roger was asked to go on a two-hour trip to a bush village where the people lived who had not heard about Christ or His truth. (And you know, wherever Roger goes, I go.) I asked one of the missionaries what I should wear since I wanted to be culturally correct. I had on a long brown and gold African dress I had been given. It went to my ankles and I had sandals on my feet. He said that I would be just fine with sandals because the natives clear all grass around the huts, so they can see snakes if they come. Great! I was set.

We started out to our destination on a paved road, which quickly became a dirt road, which became narrower and narrower, and finally it was just a two-tire track path with tall grasses in the middle of the road. Not far along the talk about spitting cobras began. No problem, I was reassured. We were in the safety of the van. At that moment, the aging van plunged into a big pothole filled with muddy water. We were stuck. The men tried rocking the van back and forth without being successful at getting out of the mud hole. I stood there watching and being amused. (Screaming wouldn't be any good.) The driver casually commented, "I think we are going to have to walk the final mile."

I in my spiffy open toed sandals and I knew that the spitting cobras--who spit twenty feet and blind people could now have me for lunch.

The stories of John the Baptist losing his head and Jonah and that whale instantly came to mind. I always go through the dramatic struggles with trust...then the van bumped out of the hole just like *that*, and as though nothing had happened at all, we moved on to the village of people waiting to hear about God's love, a love I think I just experienced. Just another usual day in the jungle.

We stood around for quite a bit just chatting with some villagers–no one was in a hurry--and I asked when things would begin. "When everyone gets here." I was told that people were coming from miles around. Some would have walked for eight hours to get to the village where they knew that God's message would be given.

But at just the right time one of the scantily dressed village men blew a huge conch shell as though he were auditioning for Carnegie Hall. That was the signal for all the people to gather who had been coming from the nearby villages. The locals had constructed a canopy of leaves and sticks that were attached to four tall poles for a chapel.

We don't know what happened in the hearts of the people that day, but God was there along the way. As Roger spoke and was translated by a missionary, the Basenji (barkless) dogs and the barely clad children, kept running in and out of the sanctuary of leaves. Not a problem for the crowd. And not a spitting cobra to be seen. The people seemed interested in Roger's talk. The translator, a very sharp ABC student probably helped the talk be more relevant. The very fat village chief did fall asleep during the meeting, but he awoke before it was over.

We were invited to then eat at one of the mud hut homes. We were to be the guests of honor. Such an honor I don't need. What will they give us to eat, and do I really want to eat it? "No" was my mental answer, but to be gracious and acceptable to this friendly, generous people we said, "Yes". We arrived at the hut and were invited in. The only things in the hut were a rickety table and two very rickety chairs. Why not more? We were told that as honored guests we would eat alone.

But what were we going to eat. I had heard about some tribes that spit in their food to give it flavor. Yuck. I really didn't want to eat the food. We were told the menu was goat's meat and cassava greens over rice. That didn't sound too bad. We ate alone attempting to be cheerful in the mud hut while the host and a crowd of people stood outside looking through the windows and door smiling and offering us more. Would you believe I had seconds? It was delicious, but I decided not to ask for their recipe nor inquire about the ingredients.

As a parting gift they gave us a live chicken to take back with us. I kept saying, "Thank you, thank you, but, no you keep it." One of the missionaries quickly whispered that we had to take it, or it would be impolite and insult the host, so I reached out and clutched the chicken by the neck. Thanks a lot, Roger. When we got in the van the missionaries said to just throw the clucking chicken under the seat. We did and the chicken cluck, cluck, clucked all the way home. She was as unnerved as we. She was made into great soup for the students the next day. How's that for another cross-cultural experience?

The cost of discipleship does not always mean sacrificing your life. But it could be as simple as eating foods that are downright scary to eat or being around green mambas.

I can do all things through Christ who strengthens me. Philippians 4:13

YOUR STORY

_____
_____
_____
_____

Chapter 16

A STRANGE HELP

Our household often included exchange students from around the world. We love the cultural differences and the times to share our faith. There was one student who created a special memory. Monica was a German who wanted to have an experience working with youth in the United States. Unfortunately, a few weeks before she came, our youth leader left to go back to school. Since I had worked for Young Life and majored in Christian Education, I was a quick substitute at the last minute. It turned out that we were a great team. She was relational and great at detail. I was relational and good at the big picture and organizational ideas. We had so much fun working together and seeing the high school group grow over the summer.

Every Wednesday evening, we had a young singles' Bible study at our home. Monica particularly felt at home with the group and everyone loved her.

One day while Monica was bike riding, a car backed out of the driveway, hit her and threw her across the street. Her femur was broken, and she was rushed to the hospital. She would heal but how would she pay for her hospital bills? She had no money. Her job in American was a faith journey. Not only that, Monica wanted to go to the U.S Center for World Missions in California for graduate study. She had little money for that and now that would be spent on medical care.

We found out that the car that hit her had insurance. Probably this would cover her medical expenses. Maybe all we will have to do is contact their insurance company and presto, the money would come. Wrong. She called and called the insurance company and they had many stalling techniques.

But here is where God came along the way! The next Wednesday night at our singles' Bible study a new young lawyer came. He was not a believer, but there were a number of sharp young men and women in the group. During the time for our prayer requests Monica asked us to please pray that the insurance company would pay for her broken leg. We did of course, but after the prayer this young lawyer said, "It will be a long time before they pay, if they ever do, unless you have a lawyer call." Hmmm! Then he said the amazing words. "Do you want me to call the insurance company for you?" Of course, Monica said, "Yes." The next day he got all the necessary information and called from our house. He told them what firm he was from and that he was checking on why Monica had not heard from then? He said all this with a very stern voice. They told him they would be sending a check soon. Done! Of course, we thanked him profusely. How great of him to go out on a limb like that having only met us the night before. We did ask what he thought they might pay her. He thought about $3500 - $4000. That would cover the medical expenses nicely. When he left we jumped up and down and hugged each other.

Four days later Monica, Roger and I were sitting eating dinner when the doorbell rang. In walked our young lawyer friend smiling. In his hand he was carrying a check for Monica. It was not $3,500.00 but $9,000. On top of that incredible gift, this young lawyer said: I have never received insurance coverage this fast or been given so much for this type of injury. Your God must have answered your prayers. That situation not only paid for Monika's bills, but helped her get to graduate school. But the best part was our young lawyer came to faith in Christ because of this event along the way.

Beware in your prayers, above everything else, of limiting God, not only by unbelief, but by fancying that you know what He can do. Andrew Murray

YOUR STORY

_____
_____
_____
_____

Chapter 17

ANGELS?

One Fall evening a few years ago, while my husband was busily back home, I was leaving my New Jersey family's home driving our five-year-old Audi with a sign on the license plate that read, "Please forgive me for having such a nice car. We got a great deal on it." It was dusk. I really shouldn't have started out for a twelve-hour journey alone. I was about forty-five minutes on my way when all the warning lights on the dash flashed on...not a good sign I knew, as though I were an MIT grad. I looked for a gas station. None. It quickly began to dawn on me that I was in a city known as having one of the country's greatest crime rates. I had a sociology degree and had read about aggressive gangs and economic unrest in inner cities. Plus, I have a PhD in "over-active imagination." (I was an honor student in that category.)

Obviously, I had a decision to make, either have my car grind to a halt on the highway in a few minutes or venture off the next ramp into the ravages of the *Forbidden City*.

"Lord, please, please help me find a gas station and keep me safe." As I circled off the ramp, I finally saw a dimly lit gas station. (I must confess that not all my prayers are answered that quickly.) I experienced a great sense of relief, but at the same time realized that the station didn't have a repair garage. Plus, the station wasn't open. With no apparent other choices, I pulled into the station hoping someone would come and know what was wrong with my car. Before I got out of the car a young, handsome man walked up to my window in a suit. Being my usual uncertain self, I opened the window just a crack and explained to the young man that all my dashboard warning lights had just gone on.

"Open your hood, let me take a look." I obediently obeyed. After a long moment (my anxiety was in check) he walked back to my window and said to me "Your serpentine belt, which runs the air conditioner, the generator and everything else, is broken and gone."

"What should I do?"

"Drive across the street to the truck stop and give him this number for the belt," He seemed to know the right number. "And be careful cause the truck stops are not too safe at night. Luckily, there's no traffic at this time." (It was now dark. Oh, why hadn't I left earlier? How come my husband doesn't take better care of our car!
Pity and anger come easily when one is scared.)

I asked the young man, "Are you an angel?" He smiled.

I wondered why he came to my window. There was no one else around that I could see. He didn't seem to be a worker at the gas station, nicely dressed, and I had just turned off the engine when he came to the window. And, now that I look back, he knew exactly what to do for my car. How did all that happen?

After looking both ways before crossing the highway, just like Mom always said, I crossed the empty street and entered the truck stop. I was expecting to be jumped any time by some grizzly looking truck driver at any moment. (Now, how do you like my imagination?) But, no, what I found was a very polite man ready to help. He looked to see if he had the numbered belt, that his seeming friend across the street had written down. "Nope, sorry," he said as he returned, "I don't have that belt," I was crestfallen. Then he added, "But give me a second and I'll call Pep Boys to see if they have one." Wow, everyone was going the extra mile.

He came back and said, "Go right away. Your car can easily limp its way there and Joe said he'd put the belt on for you and send you on your way. Hurry though, because Pep Boys closes in fifteen minutes." He gave me clear directions—just around the corner, turn left and at the light, it's right there." He walked me to my car and opened the door and said, "God bless you, lady!"

A moment ago, I was a frightened victim at a truck stop filled with dangerous, ready to pounce goblins and demons, but then, a very helpful man who had solved my problem, walked me to my car and said, *"God bless you, lady."*

He must have been another angel. Isn't it great the way God takes care of his children -even those with broken serpentine belts? I drove slowly and carefully around the corner to Pep Boys. In fifteen minutes I was "On the road again."

God brings us serendipitous moments to encourage us and make us smile—even on desolate roads on our way home. Sometimes we also can be the angel who ministers to people. People who are frightened and are trying to find *their* way to their eternal home.

Something that I have found helpful: keep letters and thank you notes that people have written to me reminding me of How God used me to intervene or offer a caring word or hug during a tough or *lost* time. I can look back frequently to be reminded that, yes, God has used me to impact other lives for His Kingdom, and certainly and blessedly, God has used others to show me *my way home.*

"The Lord is my shepherd, I shall not want. …Even though I walk through the valley of the shadow of death, I will fear no evil, for you are with me. Psalm 23: 1,4

YOUR STORY OF UNEXPECTED HELP

_____
_____
_____
_____
_____
_____
_____

Chapter 18

A SPECIAL GIFT

Two of my wiser, older siblings, impaled me greatly as I developed my decorating skills. One brother was an artist. My sister was a compulsive interior decorator. Her husband never knew where the furniture would be when he returned home from work, but he always said, "great job. Kid." Not only do I now find great pleasure in decorating and rearranging my house, but I also get springtime antsy when I start digging in the loamy, wonderful soil--even when it's under my nails. My goal always is to make our home and the sloping-into-the- woods backyard into a welcoming pleasure of color, comfort and meditative relaxation for our guests and family. I can sing, "I Come to the Garden Alone."

So, one spring I began to stroll around our home, win my new mukluks. I began planning for my next garden extravaganza. The hydrangeas had already started to blossom. The mountain laurel and holly trees were taking deep spring breaths as they nestled at the side of the house--placed just in the right spots. The hot pink impatiens boarders were ready to pop.

As I looked at the area at the side of our house, I paused. Hmm, wouldn't it be nice if we had a rustic, stone path that wound down the hill? Stepping stones. Yes, of course! The path would seductively lead to an inviting place, a glen, a reverie. I did another deep *hmmm*.

I dropped my new hoe and rake and went inside and looked in my bookmarked *Home & Garden* magazines to get some inspiration--which was something my now white haired, brother always recommended.

I finally found the magazine at the bottom of a stack of garden books A wrought iron swing with an iron trellis arching over it. Oh, just think, there would be an intoxicating Carolina jasmine flowing over the canopy. Yes, that was it. A swing!

But where would summer guests put their iced coffee or mint tea while lounging there? Oh, I know...a low-slung bird bath covered with a round of double thick, glass. That was it! Thank you, Martha Stewart.

After a month of strenuous gardening and shopping, just looking for the right pieces and placing all of them just where they belonged, I stepped back and looked at my finished masterpiece. But, no, there was something missing. With a flash of inspiration, or divine guidance, or both, I drew a circle with a stick that surrounded the swing set. It extended about six feet on both sides. There would be room for more plants, more flowers and more small bushes (I'll choose them later) within the area, making the yard even more perfect.

It turned out beautifully. Thank you, Lord, for all your creation -- especially *Home & Garden*. I spent my summer mornings there, and many years afterwards, just having a time of quiet and reading and praying. Daily I reveled in: *He restores my soul.*

Then one balmy, beautiful day a gardener pulled his truck into our driveway. He was charming and wise. He pointed out that the big hickory tree across from my beautiful swing was dead and needed to be cut down. *He may have been charming, but the devil was visiting my garden.*

"How much would that cost?" I asked not wanting to know the answer.

"One thousand dollars," he answered, without even a calculating blink.

"Thank you, but no thanks. We don't have a thousand dollars just to remove a tree." And I didn't blink either.

I told Roger when he returned from playing tennis. His response was the same as mine. But there stood the dead tree threatening to fall on my beautiful swing and garden. It probably won't fall for a long, long while I reassured myself...will it? But as I looked at the tree and the way it was leaning, I knew that if it fell it would be dead center on top of my wonderful, wrought iron swing that had my awesome flowers dancing around it.

Nah, it won't fall, I said to myself. It is a tall, strong hickory tree. It just died. The roots are still strong.

Have you heard the word, *tornado*? Well, I told myself, tornadoes never come to the mountain where we live. Little did I have a clue that a few miles west of us, and a few days after the friendly arborist had doomed our dead tree, that huge gusts of wind, lasting only a few seconds crossed our paths. (I stole Scarlet O'Hara's, "Fiddle dee dee.")

The next morning the spring sun was out and beginning to warm the air. I walked out on the back deck to look once more at my beautiful swing and garden. But a huge, evil had intruded in our Eden. Our aged, giant, dead hickory lay sprawled across the lawn, a mere six inches from our swing.

"Roger, come look at the gift God gave us last night!" I shouted! Behold, that too-expensive-to-be removed tree, now had its limbs and trunk smashed and splayed on the ground. Nothing was destroyed in my beautiful garden! "Thank you, Lord," I breathed.

Later, two young men stopped by and cheerfully said, "Hey. we heat our home with firewood. Could we have that tree? There is nothing better than hickory. We'll cart off all the tree and branches if you'll let us have the wood."

"Wow, oh, yes, of course!" I said with a little too much glee. And if I didn't slow down the enthusiasm, they'd think about charging me for the removal. "Why, you very nice young men, of course you may cart away that pesky old tree."

At the end of the great job they cheerfully did, they even left all the smaller logs for our fire place. We'll be log-rich for the next two years.

Now. How much did that all cost? Zero!

Again, we saw God's loving hand along the way.

My mother, who always had an old, fitting Scottish proverb to quote, used to say, "You can never out give the Lord. You shovel it out and He shovels it in and his shovel is bigger than yours.

"And my God will meet all your needs according to his glorious riches in Christ Jesus. Philippians 4:19

YOUR STORY OF GOD'S PROVISION-

_____
_____
_____
_____
_____

Chapter 19

HOW WILL I GET HOME?

Roger and I planned another trip visiting some of the Entrust staff. This time it was to Budapest, Hungary. We were to be available to pastor the missionaries at Entrust's annual Field Staff Development Conference. All the European staff would be there.

One week before departure I was getting out of bed and felt an ever so slight twinge in my lower back. That "slight twinge" increased to painful immobility by the end of the day. I could not walk without excruciating pain shooting across my lower back. It felt like my back would snap every time I tried to move. It was one of those pains that gave me the feeling that I couldn't walk over the edge of the carpet, let alone try to get into or out of bed. So how in the world could I ever take a trip to Eastern Europe? Maybe it will go away in a day or two.

Not so!

Cleverly Roger took me to a back specialist. He looked me over...humm... gave me a shot, some free samples of pain medicine and *voila* in a couple days the pain was...well, almost gone. I did mention to the doctor that I planned on leaving for Eastern Europe in a few days. He gave me a shocked look.

. "No, I don't think that's a good idea." I thought for a second and decided we would go.

Surprise, surprise. The next few days my back felt pretty good, so off we went to Europe for a month. After the conference we had planned to visit our missionaries in Romania, Russia and Austria.

As you may have experienced, jet-lag wipes out a person's normal sleeping schedule for a few days. The usual stateside wake up time comes in the middle of the morning at your new location. So, in the pitch black of the night I woke up and decided to see what time it was. Without turning on the bed table light, so I wouldn't awaken Roger, I got up, leaned over to see the clock on the night table. Pow! My back stiffened, locked, and gave me horrendous pain. I couldn't move. The doctor's voice in my head, "I wouldn't recommend traveling" was harsh and scolding.) I was locked in a bent position. "Roger, ROGER! I can't move! My back has gone out...aaagh," I screeched. A startled Roger, in alarm mode, lifted me very carefully to the couch. I was heavy, I could not move, but I could sit. There was nothing to do at 4:00 in the morning. What might help: heat...ice...dying?... I sat still hoping to ward off pain until the sun came up.

Roger had a scheduled meeting at 7:00 am. What was I going to do? In a wash of self-pity and hurt I didn't want to be left alone. What if I had to go to the bathroom? Someone had to be here to help me move. I could hardly move. Moving at all was very painful. (I was doing a Tony Award performance about being alone.) So, long-suffering Roger pulled me up gently from the couch. While I moaned and groaned, he helped dress me. My moving was a slow shuffle.

I decided to go to the breakfast room where I could sit and at least talk To people. There was an elevator near our room. So painstakingly, with the emphases on the pain, I shuffled to the elevator and then sat down at the closest table in the dining room. This was going to be a long day. Maybe I should have stayed home. *Ya think?* Roger went off to his meeting.

After about five minutes of severe pain and discomfort, (There was no way to get comfortable.), three of the women who work in the Entrust home office came by and said, "We've come to pray for you." I was grateful, but surprised they had already heard about my crisis, but Roger had spread the word. They circled about me and placed their hands on my shoulders. Each one prayed. As they were praying I felt a rippling down my vertebra. A strange sensation.
The women headed off. I sat for a few moments, not moving. Then I had to find a restroom but wasn't sure I could stand, let alone walk the twenty feet to the room. I gingerly pulled myself up and really, to my shock, I had no difficulty walking, not one symptom of back problems. "Thank you, Lord!" I had never experience a healing, (so much for my faith), but I was like the man on the stretcher, whose friends lowered their paralytic friend down through the roof for Jesus to heal him. I believed the story but had never experienced it.

I haven't had a back problem since, and all my worries about "*How I was going to get home*" was answered by our powerful God as he used three believing women, Leslie Smith, Kathy Queen, and Lynn Ebert.

"God is an infinite and immense being, whose center is everywhere, and whose circumference is nowhere" The *Secret Key to Heaven* - Thomas Brooks

YOUR STORY

_____
_____
_____

Chapter 20

A TURNING POINT

Here I was a sophomore at a Christian College. A college where one went to chapel five times a week and heard the best of Christian speakers challenging you to be God's representative where ever you were and in every area of your life.

I did want that to be true in my life but there were those areas I passed over with the thought, "It's not that big of a deal and nobody's perfect." No one will really pay any attention to my little foibles and actually no one will ever know. Anyway, it doesn't hurt anyone." You might have noticed a bit of rationalization there. I was just fooling myself. But because God loves me, he began to do some house cleaning in my heart and mind. That process is not easy and can cause extreme embarrassment and is often costly.

As I listened to various chapel talks, God began to convict me of "little" sins in my life that were really caused by laziness and a lack of discipline. Too often I took the easy way out. The real word for it is 'cheating'. My rationale was I'm not hurting anyone. I'll only do it this time. But God began to make that kind of thinking more and more uncomfortable for me. That process was not easy. Changing long time patterns are costly and hard.

As I listened in chapel I was slowly becoming more and more aware of these "little" sins in my life. But I continued to rationalize my actions. For example, one time I did all the homework for an eighty-page handbook that we had worked on all year. But now it was time to organize it and put it in shape for future use. Being quite good at rationalization and not leaving enough time to put the paper together well, I thought, "I have done the homework that's the important part. The final compilation is just busy work" So I took a friend's handbook from a previous year and pretty much made it mine. I did all the real work and using her finished paper to type would sure take a lot less time.

After I turned in the handbook, God would not let me put my cheating out of my mind. I remember so clearly trying to keep rationalizing. "I will never do it again, so I don't have to confess. But God would not let me take the easy way out. My professor for this course had a sister who also was one of my teachers. So, if I confessed, both teachers would probably know. But, I knew I had to admit what I had done. I had a hard time thinking of facing her, so I decided to write her a note and mail it in the campus post office. As I stood at the mailbox knowing that when I let that letter drop, I couldn't get it back. What would the professor do? I could get an "F" for the semester and maybe even get kicked out of the school. I held the note at the slot for quite a while and then with a final release, I let it drop. It was gone and now the consequences. Actually, my first emotion was relief. I had been obedient to the Lord. That felt very good.

But then I had to face my professor in class the next day. Waiting for that class was a stomach cramping experience. I embarrassingly went into class, but nothing was said. However, when my handbook was handed back to me a few days later she only lowered my grade from a B to a C. The only note on the cover was, "Joy, you need to ask yourself why you did this?"

Wow! That was a gracious punishment. But considering her question became a turning point in my studying. I had played around with school mostly having fun. But now I began to realize that these years of study were a gift from God and I needed to honor him as I studied. The Bible tells us to do our work as doing it for the Lord. That began a huge change in how I studied. It also caused my grades to greatly improve. A new joy and freedom welled up in my relationship with God. I finally became a student, and in addition, my walk with Christ had new vibrancy and reality. Those steps of obedience changed my life in so many ways. Obedience to God seems to do that.

Your Story of a Turning Point in your life

_____
_____
_____
_____
_____
_____

Chapter 21

ALONE

I was a newlywed, but I had no husband.

No husband, because Roger, my newly "I Do" husband, had left two weeks after we were married for a cruise aboard the USS San Pablo. He was a brilliant, charming ensign for Uncle Sam. The cruise was to last two months, a long, lonely time for a newlywed. Our honeymoon cottage was a motel room in Hampton Beach, New Hampshire, near Portsmouth, the San Pablo's home port.

I had to find a job. Finding work was important for me to make enough money to help Roger through three years in seminary. I had just left Young Life staff, working with teenagers, where I had saved zero dollars. And I had just produced a great wedding. What was I going to do? The anxious stomach syndrome began to take over. I had been a Christian Education and Psychology major in college but none of the Hampton Beach churches were big enough to hire a C.E. Director. So where did my qualifications fit in, I wondered?

My new task was to impress my absent husband that I could

be financially helpful. Maybe I could find something at the "Y", being creative with teens, or perhaps teaching school. After all I had taken several courses in education.

Who was I kidding? Who'd hire me? My confidence and self-image were already tattered. But each morning I went through the motions of looking for work. It was June. So, I went to an elementary school that was advertising an opening for a third-grade teacher. Nervously, and not expecting too much, I went for an interview. The young principal introduced himself: "Good morning, I'm Harry Johnson." He had a non-threatening approach and smiled a lot. "Tell me about your experience teaching."

Smiling, I said, "None." (This was going to be a quick interview. but I plunged on.) "Well, um, my previous job was...." I filled in the details of my Young Life work. He continued with the interrogation: "What are the characteristics of junior aged kids?" I responded confidently, sounding as if I had written the basic text book on Little People Eager to Learn. I could do that because in my Christian Education field work in college I worked with junior aged children, I had carefully studied the mental, physical, social, emotional, spiritual characteristics of that age group. I was able to rattle off the unique characteristics of third and fourth graders like I had written a Pulitzer winning book on the subject. The pedagogy came off my tongue without a blip. I was on a roll. I sensed the Lord was at work.

The principal seemed a bit impressed. Casually he just mentioned that there was another woman (uh oh) interviewing for the job, but added that he thought, "You might just be the better choice."

"I need to look at your college transcript. Mmm, um hum, good, (he read on), good." He said my Church History courses could count for the history requirement, my Christian Education of Children for education. (I was really liking this man. I sat up straighter.) He thought my course work fulfilled the school's educational requirements, and he'd like to hire me. My heart skipped. "Oh, but there are two stipulations: you'll need to take a course on teaching elementary math, and a children's science course before school starts." Wow! I quickly enrolled in Monmouth College near my home in New Jersey where I'd be spending the summer.

I could hardly wait to tell Roger! They hired a person who didn't major in Elementary Education, didn't have any school practice teaching, or had ever taught. And it was a good New England school Was God in on this?

As I looked ahead to the Fall, I still was very nervous about teaching, since I knew nothing about teaching third graders and contemporary pedagogy? Not only that, I knew no one in New Hampshire.

I shouldn't have feared because God had that all worked out, but I didn't know his plan yet. Thankfully, my sister and my brother arrived in late August to help me find and decorate a modest apartment. It was a small place just a block from the beach. A little grocery store was on the corner where I could buy anything I might want. The three of us siblings got busy decorating and created something that even Martha Stewart would have applauded, well, maybe just have given a wry smile.

As my brother, Paul, and sister, Ruth, who had worked extremely hard, were about to leave, we were standing outside my apartment enjoying the fresh sea air and saying our good-byes. It was a typically dazzling, early autumn day. Strangely, the pay phone booth on the corner began ringing. It continued ringing and ringing. Reluctantly, and being nosey, I picked up the phone, and in a curious tone said: "Hello."

The person on the other end, asked if I were, Joy? *Joy!* No one in New Hampshire knew me--other than God--and no one could possibly know I had just moved there. Who knew what the number of the pay phone was? Was this a radio show joke or a scene from a Hitchcock thriller?

"Hi, Joy, I'm the wife of one of the officers on Roger's ship. I'm calling to ask if you could come to a picnic this evening at our home." Was this a joke? Just because I'm curious I said "yes" and got all the directions. When I told my brother and sister, we all laughed at the incredibleness of God. We said happy good byes.

It turned out in the next few days that I was learning that navy wives take care of each other when their husbands are out at sea; but I still never found out how Claire (my new best friend) had contacted me by means of a pay phone outside my newly rented apartment. Needless to say, I still am amazed. The party that evening was great fun and I was instantly welcomed into a new community.

But wait. There was still a heavenly Father watching over a stranded, lonely newlywed. The first day of school orientation, I was nervous, no, scared to death. I had to pretend that I knew how to teach school. I sat in the parking lot and prayed about my scary day. What happened to practice teaching and mentors? I prayed I might find a friend or someone I might even know. (Not likely.) I went into the teachers' lounge crowded with teachers and tables full of refreshments. I kept smiling, hoping someone would talk to me. (Roger, I hate the navy.) Then I spotted this young guy who looked strangely familiar. Hesitantly, I walked over to him and said, "You look familiar to me. Do I look familiar to you?" Sounded like a come on. He quickly, so like a guy, said, "No". How embarrassed I felt. I was planning to crawl under one of the kid's desk in the room. Roger, where are you?

Trying again I asked, "Where did you go to college?" "Barrington, a little college in New England and then to Wheaton College" "Oh, that's interesting. I went to both of those schools," I had tears in my eyes, tears, because it was such a wonderful answer to a prayer not spoken. Another teacher, his wife I discovered, came wandering over, probably to check out who this Lorelei was talking to her husband. I quickly discovered she had also gone to the same two colleges. We comically broke into singing our school songs.

That night and so many other nights, while Roger was away for *six* months--not two months--this wonderful couple invited me over for dinner. They also invited me to participate in a great Bible study lead by the pastor of their very, friendly church. I began to attend regularly. *"His eye is on the sparrow and I know He watches me."*

Back then, now many years ago, I was so scared, but I discovered that God was always there.

Trust in the Lord with all your heart, lean not to your own understanding, in all your ways acknowledge Him and He will direct your path. Proverbs 3:5,6

Your Story of God helping you when you felt alone or not ready for what was ahead.

_____
_____
_____
_____
_____

Chapter 22

JOHN HAMPTON EDDIE

On the shores of Gitche Gumee

By the shining Big-Sea-Water,
Stood the wigwam of Nokomis,
Daughter of the Moon, Nokomis.

Dark behind it rose the forest,
Rose the black and gloomy pine-trees,
Rose the firs with cones upon them;

Bright before it beat the water.
Beat the clear and sunny water,
Beat the shining Big-Sea-Water.

Hiawatha's Childhood

Longfellow's Poems

Throughout my childhood I quoted Longfellow's poem, often wondering where I'd learned it. In *our* tradition the only thing worth memorizing was the Bible.

"Mom. Where ever did I learn that poem?

"From our yard man?

"You mean, Mr. Hampton?"

"Yes. And do you remember that he also made you and your brother birthday cakes each year. And you always got a special cake for each of our presidents' birthdays--Washington, Jefferson, Roosevelt, all of them. There was always a cake. And they were delicious."

I have nothing but good memories of Mr. Hampton even though I was eight or nine back then when he was always around our big Victorian house. He was a tall, thin, handsome, elegant and elderly man in his mid-sixties, who always spoke softly. He was the consummate gentleman.

My mother told me that Mr. Hampton had been a casualty of the 1930's depression years. He was a vagrant drunk when he staggered into my father's Rescue Mission in New Jersey. Through Christ he got his life together. After several years of sobriety and helpfulness he obviously showed traits of having come from a very cultured background. His grammar was elegant. But there was no personal history.

Mr. Hampton helped clean our large home that was often a ruckus of four kids, did the gardening (he loved that) and, of course, made those celebratory cakes. He seemed a member of the family who went home each night. When the family retreated to the sea shore for the summer (No one wanted to get polio in those years, so we were off to the beach.) Mr. Hampton (no one called him John) had already been to our little tent/cabin to clean it and set out our second-hand furniture. (After all it was the war years). Then he would return to our home, take down the drapes and clean them, remove the rugs, hang them outside and take the rug beater to them. Windows were shined to a crystal sparkle. Mattresses were turned. On and on, summer after summer. Oh, he tended our gardens in his spare time.

Obviously, my family trusted him completely.

At the end of one summer Mr. Hampton was continuing one of his impressive routines of replanting our spring tulip bulbs. He had just completed one of his favorite tasks when his heart gave out and he slumped on his well-tended garden and silently died.

Who was John Hampton? Did he have a family? Who needed to be contacted and informed? A search ensued. Pieces of John's story, from sequestered letters and legal papers found in his foot locker, began to create a very different person. Eventually an elderly brother was located. He promptly identified the body and arranged for its interment in the family plot.

We were told that John's full name was John Hampton Eddy. He was born into a wealthy family who lived on Park Avenue, New York; he was educated in The Groton School, a prestigious New England, private boarding school, where Franklin Roosevelt had been his classmate.

A wealthy relative of John's had died and left the young, college graduate a family fortune. John proceeded to squander his largess with a generous hand. Hard drinking and horse racing absorbed much of his time and money. However, along the way, he established some impressive business connections, once being a broker in Wall Street, and again occupying an executive position in Washington during the Taft administration. Given the roaring 20's intemperate drinking habits, John was caught. The Depression Era took its toll on John. The brilliant, wealthy man soon earned the title of Down and Out. As a wandering vagrant he landed in Trenton, was picked up and taken to the police station. "I'm only looken' for a plach to stay for the night," he slurred. He was referred to the City Rescue Mission. (My father was the Executive Director).

After sobering up and having some sleep, there emerged a significant transformation in habits and outlook on his life. He never drank again from the night he entered the Mission and was soon transformed by the message of Christ.

His private life and history were his own and he never spoke of the details. He was too ashamed to return home and we became the family for whom he made birthday cakes and from whom he received deep appreciation and love.

I have warm, fond memories still in my adult life of how the power of God changed his life and how that new life brought such fun and delight and good into my childhood. Thank you, John, you were an important part of my growing childhood. I look forward to greeting you in heaven by *the bright and shiny Waters of Gitche Gumee.*

What shall it profit a man to gain the whole world but forfeit his soul. Matthew 16:26.

MY STORY OF A PERSON WHO MEANT MUCH TO ME:

_____
_____
_____
_____
_____
_____

Chapter 23

GOD WORKS ALL THINGS FOR GOOD

I was thirteen when my father decided to open a summer restaurant just three blocks from the East Coast's warm sunny beaches. If you had known my dad and my Scottish immigrant mom, that meant the whole family would be working at our little eatery named Keating's Cozy Cottage. This decision also included getting up every morning before the sun was up and heading off to work when the sun was creeping down in the West. How awful for a teenager! We did get off 2:00-4:30 every afternoon. That was just enough time to run to the beach and body surf a few waves.

We got off if our lunch customers left on time and no one came to our door one minute before 2:00 p.m. My father's favorite words to people who came to our restaurant late were, "We're closed, but what would you like?" Of course, one family member, which too often was me, was chosen to stay over time. I was not a happy camper.

I remember at age thirteen how terrible I was at waitressing. I would forget napkins, silverware or water. How I hated it all. Didn't my parents know I was young and wanted to have fun instead of working. On top of that when a waitress got sick and didn't show up guess who was the fill-in waitress. The one positive outcome of the whole work thing was that I earned money! Of course, my mean old parents opened a bank account for my future college years. Never let it be said I was spoiled.

As an adult and as my life developed, I realized how God used all those years of running around serving people in our restaurant to highly develop in me an important skill, multi-tasking under pressure. That skill made it easier to put on all the high school camps and adult retreats my husband and I developed and ran. We were busy with church schedules and children's schedules, but I seemed to be able to deal with all of that and at the same time plan a retreat and be planning a dinner for friends. I thought, "Thanks Mom and Dad for the gift you gave me of waitressing even though I was so awful at it. You should have fired me.

As I reflect back I realize my heavenly Father had put me through hoops and loops that were always meant to build me up and teach me important lessons. He often uses our parents in the process.

What is God trying to develop in you right now? *We know that in all things God works for the good of those who love Him" Romans 8:28.* "

It is said of Christ, *"He learned obedience from what he suffered" Hebrew 5:8.*

Your Story of God helping you when you felt alone or not ready for what was ahead.

Your story of God working things out

_____
_____
_____
_____
_____
_____

Chapter 24

THE LIE

We were off to Ecuador. A two-week mission trip with some of our travel-eager parishioners. Ecuador isn't far from Brazil, which when I was a teen, was one of the places I thought God would send me to be a missionary; and I was sure God would send me my travel orders when He and I were ready. Those esoteric forests I fantasized would be places, I naively imagined, where most certainly I would romantically live in a tree hut with wild natives and jaguars prowling beneath me--eager to kill me. Of course, I was willing--if God so chose me--to be the next heroic martyr. There would be books and films about my impressive life. Oh, how young I was.

Ecuador wasn't Brazil and should be easy. I was going to a place to work on a missionary compound in a safe place. *Did I say in a safe place?* Oh, maybe a tarantula or a boa constrictor just lurking somewhere outside our sleeping quarters. Easy.

But no one told me about the road from Quito, Ecuador to Shell-- the place where we were headed. I assumed Shell was a quaint, little oil drilling town owned by the Dutch. Curious, I thought, how come everyone called the Shell Road the *Road from Hell*. I gave it no thought until a roadside merchant tried to sell me a tee shirt with the logo, "I survived the Shell Road." Whatever could *that* mean?

What it meant was a six-hour bumpy, treacherous ride to our destination. Up a narrow hill, twisting up an extremely high mountain road with 1000-foot drops with no walls or railinsgs to keep a car from going off into an abyss. There were no turn around areas. Two long, rickety pine boards had to be used to cross those places where the road just disappeared into nowhere that we could see. Our missionary, who was middle aged but already grey, said in a rather matter of fact way that she had safely traveled this road before, but lots of people and cars had fallen over the side before. She loved our reactions. And I began to wonder if she was really a Christian.

I was struggling with the idea of repentance when an eighteen-wheeler careened from around a treacherous corner heading right towards us. Where in the world was that monstrous wheeler going to pass, and why was that huge truck on our narrow, scary road? That wasn't really very nice of our old missionary lady, who looked back at me and grinned, as she said, "This isn't your usual super highway." She instantly transmogrified into the decrepit, Snow White witch of movie fame. "Sorry, she said, "It's the only road to get to Shell."

Hardly looking back, our seemingly untroubled driver began looking for any indentation or crevice in the mountain that she could pull into, so the truck could scrape past us.

I was praying, my heart was pounding, and my mind was saying, "Why in the world did I come on this trip?" The truck scraped by. My head was in my lap. I gasped, "Thank you Lord." But the thought that pushed away all that thanking was, "Oh, my gosh, we're going to have to go back on this road!" *Lord, please keep us safe.* Needless to say, the trip was a terrifying six hours. And they call this Shell Road a *road*. It was a dry, rocky river bed next to deadly 1000-foot drop offs. That's what it was!

We finally made it to our destination with a great sense of relief and the lurking dread of a return trip.

The Shell compound was small and cozy like some childhood summer camp. Thank you, Lord, and I'm sorry for all my anxiety and fear. Some of the missionary children had cute little black monkeys as their pets which were fun. Then one of the perverse missionaries said with a smile, "Look up there in the rafters." I saw something crawling around. "What is it?" I didn't want to know.

"Tarantulas!"

"You're kidding!"

"No, I'm not. They're pretty harmless."

"Yea, Right!" They were right outside my open window, a window that really didn't close. You can bet the first two nights I had trouble going to sleep thinking about those tarantulas crawling across my face. Finally, I was so tired I fell asleep and to my knowledge those creatures weren't interested in my face.

We had an incredible ten days of work and fun with the missionaries. Roger and I mostly turned an open attic into two bedrooms.

One of our team tuned all the pianos in the area…which greatly helped times of worship. Others helped in the hospital.

Finally, it was time to return to Shell Road. "Oh, Lord, please be with us as we travel the six hours back." I was all prayed up when the news came that there was a strike by the farmers along the road. The road was closed. Hey, hooray! That was great news. But how were we going to get back to Quito to catch our plane?

No problem, the legendary MAF pilots (Missionary Aviation Fellowship) would fly us out in their small planes. "Oh, yes, Lord, thanks for the escape from that dreaded *Shell Road*.

The day came when we were to leave. We packed our small suitcases, hugged everyone and said we were grateful for all of their generous hospitality. We stood in the shaded hanger, waiting to board our little yet magnificent MAF plane.

"I have an announcement," said the handsome aviator. "We need your weight, so we can have the right weight of people in each plane." I was just a very tiny, little bit over weight at that time, (not much. Oh, OK 15 pounds), and I was embarrassed to tell how much I really weighed. What would a few pounds mean anyway? I fudged a little when I gave my weight. What would it matter?

The young aviator made another announcement about who would be in each of the two planes. "Oh," he said rather authoritatively, "it's very important that we have just the right weight in each plane, otherwise it could cause a crash. Make sure all your personal weights were accurate."

I was caught. (My mother told me never to lie, and here I was on the mission field and a pastor's wife as well), and now I was going to have to tell that I was heavier than I wanted anyone to know and had lied to a missionary who was spending his life in a forsaken jungle. I quietly went up to the pilot and said, "I didn't realize how important our weight was and I didn't give the accurate weight. I fudged a little, figuratively as well, and I am so sorry." (I was sure I would be sent back to my dreaded mountain cliff road.)

That young missionary now looked more angelic as he placed me in another plane. How embarrassing and what a lesson I learned. We flew in those little, wonderful planes through the mountains. We skimmed the beautiful, awesome, terrifying Shell Road. I waved. We had a smooth and beautiful flight that only took a mere hour-- incredible sights of valleys and mountains coloring the evening sky. I gave a sigh of relief, for I was still learning to trust my loving heavenly Father on my way.

"Before we can pray, "Lord, thy Kingdom come," we must be willing to pray," My Kingdom go." Alan Redpath

YOUR STORY OF BEING AFRAID OF BEING TRUTHFUL OR YOUR TELLING A "TINY" MISTRUTH.

_____
_____
_____
_____
_____
_____
_____

Chapter 25

THE "WAY INN"

It was our second summer working with youth and college students in our church on Lookout Mt., Tennessee. Last year we hadn't been particularly effective, or to be more positive, we hadn't connected with the teenagers. It takes time to get to know everyone and for students to let their guards down. We prayed and brain stormed about how we could better connect with the students. We prayed.

Tom Stark, who had led my husband, Roger, to the Lord, had mentioned that one summer he set up a summer training program for college students. He recruited Christian students from around the area and trained them to work with the youth in his church.

"Roger, why don't we do something like that!" Being a sensible pessimist, he listed all the reasons why such an idea wouldn't and couldn't work. I agreed with all his reasons. They were right on: we have no house, no college students to live in the house, and we don't have any jobs for the students, and certainly no one to chaperon a dozen college students for a summer, and then, and no, and, and…and. I was already exhausted. I felt defeated, a little despondent.

That night before turning off the nightstand light, I said, "Well, let's just pray and see what happens. If it doesn't work, we'll do something else." The next morning, I was still excited about our ideas and wanted to make our non-existent summer program happen.

First, I would need to find a dozen mature college students committed to sharing their faith, and who would be willing to come to our mountain church for the summer. I wrote a group of our college students from our former church and presented our ideas. Fifteen students signed up.

But now I had to get fifteen people summer jobs. That was going to take a small miracle. Maybe a *big* miracle! Our small town had only 5000 residents. There were very few jobs available. Then too, all the local college students would be coming home looking for jobs. Only God could intervene. Would you believe I found jobs for them all: at the country club as life guards and at the snack bar at the club, community playground attendants, and a variety of jobs at the famous Rock City tourist attraction. I tried to find jobs where high school students hung out.

Roger, still the professional skeptic, asked, "Joy, dear, where are all your college students going to live?" Hmm.

Some days later when I was getting gas, I noticed across the street from the gas station a formerly, lovely, stone house behind a stone wall on the other side of the street. It looked abandoned. The large lawn hadn't been cut in a year. Another hmm. I wondered who owned that house. I asked around and found out it belonged to someone from *our church!* "Oh, Lord, is this the house?"

I approached the owner. He looked very much like Rett Butler at Tara. He said in his most gracious southern accent, "Oh, mah dear, that tacky place'll be torn down by this time next year."

The following morning, we met so he could show me his place; surely there was a slight mist suspended above the moors, "Rett" walked me around his large property that had been in his family forever, and been through that "Damn Yankee War." I was so excited. Not only was the house large enough for my sixteen people, but the grounds were huge! "After the house is torn down and the property developed there will be thirteen lovely homes built here. We'll incorporate that natural waterfall and keep that stand of ancient trees covered with that lovely Spanish moss. If you want it for the summer, it yours. The insurance is still covered, and the utilities are connected."

Can you believe it?

Well, slow down. Now all we needed was a house parent and a cook for the students. Where in the world would we find someone like that, someone who would work for free? Not to worry! God will let me know.

Reset the scene. It just so happened that every morning a friend of mine, a single mom, would bring her boys over to my kitchen for a quick breakfast since we lived just across from the elementary school. It made it very easy for her to drop them off before she had to get to work. I enjoyed being able to help. One morning I was talking to her about our new *Tara* property and looking for someone to live in the house that would be full of high school and college students most of the time.

She quietly said, "It just so happens I need to move out of my house and have been looking for somewhere to stay. I would love to be the housemother and I've worked with youth a lot."

"Oh, Lord, you are so good." I hugged her; we laughed. I shouted, "Thank you, Lord!" I thought to myself, "God's covered everything."

Well, not yet!

We needed beds for the 15 students, furniture for all the empty rooms. Word quickly got out about our Summer Youth Project, (I can't believe how that happened, since I'm so shy and retiring) and people became excited and rallied. Someone retrieved eight bunk beds and mattresses from the Salvation Army. A friend bought new sheets and pillow cases for each bed. Since our new housemother needed a house she also needed storage for her furniture. Graciously her furniture furnished our living room, dining room and kitchen. Roger's young adult Sunday morning class also became involved. They cleaned up the scraggly yard and the neglected house that had been empty for years. Roger and I were jumping up and down and hugging each other. What a delightful sojourn. What a God who was surprising us every day.

We named the house: 'The Way Inn". A wonderful double meaning. It was to be an Inn for people to stay, and a *way* **in** the kingdom of God.

The question to be asked was: Was all the hard work and planning and moving furniture and painting walls and lining up people to help worth it? Yes, yes, yes! The Way Inn became the summer hangout for all the college and high school students on the mountain. There were fifteen Christian college students who had many chances of leading our high school students to Christ and discipling them. We also had a chance to disciple those college students. Our youth group grew from about thirty students to eighty-five. Every Monday night we had Bible teachers from Covenant College teach our mountain college students and those living in the house and our seniors in high school. The students received excellent biblical and theological teaching. It would impact them all their lives.

The young mother and her two boys had the time of their lives. We often look back to that summer as a turning point in our ministry and the high point of seeing God at work along our way.

"Faith is to believe what we do not see, and the reward of this faith is to see what we believe." St. Augustine

YOUR STORY

_____
_____
_____
_____
_____

Chapter 26

BEYOND EXPECTATIONS

My husband just retired from his last pastorate. We had been there sixteen years but to give the new pastor "free rein," we decided it would be best for us to move out to another town. So, where we would live? After much prayer and thinking, we decided to move back to Lookout Mountain, Tennessee. It was a beautiful place with woods and trails, lovely winding roads with many beautiful homes. And we still had many good friends there.

Our question was, "Would there be a house we could afford? In previous years we lived in a manse owned and provided for us by the church. We didn't have much money but perhaps we could find a fixer upper or maybe there would be a nice, but much smaller home.
Small was not ideal for the times when the whole family came to visit over the holidays. But…

Off we went to investigate the possibilities. We found a house that was the right meager price, the right layout and space but… the whole house was in bad shape. The front of the house was, in my humble opinion, ugly. Also, I wasn't sure that it could even be changed to look better. We prayed, "Lord, show us what we are to do." We asked, "How much would it cost to fix this place up?" The bathrooms were very outdated, and the kitchen cabinets were crooked. but the sizes of the rooms were good, and it had a lovely deck. Look a bit more. We found another house that was quite nice and in good shape. It was only ten years old and it had, to my delight, an outside hot tub. It was nice, but it was above our budget. My very cautious and frugal husband said, "We can do it." I almost fell over; I was so ecstatic! Then the owner said, "We are building a new home, so we won't be able to move out for three months."

Not to worry, our friends had a down stairs apartment we could use until we could move in. The apartment over looked the Tennessee River. How graciously kind of the Lord to give us such gracious friends. Ah, all was settled. The only negative was if our beautiful house in South Carolina sold quickly, then we would have to put *our* furniture in storage. More money out of our pockets. We headed back home to sell our house. In a short time, we received a call from the owners of our new potential home. "Sorry, but it will take at least eight months before you could move in. Also, we have looked over things more carefully and we feel like we need to raise the asking price for the house by $30.000."

Our first thought was, "Oh, no, what are we going to do now?" But we had walked with Christ long enough to know that "in all things God works for the good of those who love him." Yes, we were disappointed, but honestly, deep down, we really didn't want to go in debt at this time in life.

That week Nancy, a good friend from the mountain, called and said, "Can you come this weekend to look at a house I think you will like?" Nancy had been praying with us about finding a house. Nancy told us she had been watching her grandchildren play soccer and when she turned around, she saw something she hadn't noticed before. "A nice almost completed brand-new house." So, she went over and asked the builder when it would be done. "In about a week."

"Get here quickly" If you like the house, you can pick out the paint colors, hardwood floor stain, tile, carpets, chandeliers and all those things."

She asked if we could come this weekend. Oh, no, we couldn't. We had promised Roger's mother to take her to visit Roger's brother in Charleston, S.C.

Fifteen minutes later our phone rang, and Roger's mother said she wasn't feeling well and so she probably shouldn't go to Charleston.

Roger and I looked at each other--God's timing is something! We packed and headed for the mountain to see the house.

Oh, wow! The brand-new house was everything we wanted, crown moldings, enough rooms for our kids and grandchildren, high ceilings, hardwood floors, granite counter tops, brass fixtures, a nice front yard, woods in the backyard, and the landscaping went with it. I was afraid to ask the builder how much it would cost, but I did. It was $95,000 less than the other house, and under our budgeted amount for a house. Also, the timing was perfect and there would be no storage fees for our furniture. "Oh Lord, you are so gracious to us."

On top of that our house sold in South Carolina for what we asked. In a short time, we moved in to our lovely new home, just after the hardwood floors dried.

How's that for seeing God along the way? So, when circumstances seem to be going against you, stop and pray for eyes to see God's good plan.

I SAW GOD ALONG THE WAY

Your Story of God opening the doors in wonderful ways

_____
_____
_____
_____
_____
_____

Chapter 27

A KNOCK AT MY DOOR

It was a teaching job, my first. It was a new town, a naval base town, a beach resort in New Hampshire. Everything was new to me, and unfamiliar. I, a people person, was in a place, unlike the TV show, "Cheers," where no one knew my name.

I was also a new bride away from home while my husband Roger was cruising around the Caribbean docking at ports that people spend money while going on vacation. . Being a splendid and heroic lieutenant junior grade, standing at attention in a gold-encrusted, blue serge uniform in the US Navy. I was moping around feeling sorry for myself,

First day at my new job, I discovered the teachers' lounge--I hid there during classroom breaks. It was a great place where I could munch my peanut butter and jelly sandwich--with crusts extravagantly cut off. I was *the new gal on the block*. The teachers' lounge chatter was about getting to know one another. We also used the time in the lounge to commiserate about our daily struggle with the twenty-five wild stallions we had in each of our classrooms.

I met a young, blond teacher, named Carol, who was especially friendly and reached out to me, showed me around and introduced me to everyone. Roger was cruising the Caribbean and I was alone living in winter-bound New Hampshire and the school's latest hire.

There were always light hearted, gossipy chats throughout the weeks that helped me survive. But one day our conversation took on a much more serious tone as Carol was having some struggles with her husband, and she, rather directly, asked what I would do in a similar situation. Having been married for a few weeks, and still the starry-eyed bride and had not even started the first chapter of "How to Have a Terrific Marriage Without Even Trying," I gave her the only response I could give. I said, "I'm so sorry, I'll pray for you. God really loves you and He does amazing things when we turn to him."

End of conversation. I had just flunked counseling 101

Carol looked at me blankly and left.

After all, it *was* time for me to go back to my unruly class. *"Tommy, you know you're not allowed to jump on your desk. Sally, stop punching him and sit down--now!"* The class was a maelstrom of shrieking banshees, (Hey, these were my first weeks of teaching in this school--or any school.) "Everyone sit down. NOW! And fold your hands."

I did pray for Carol after class, after I'd taken several deep breaths. Several days later: Another prayer. "God open up a little door for truth to seep in to my conversation with Carol. Amen. Oh, and yes, help me to say the right things."

A few weeks passed and a similar conversation with Carol came up. "Lord Help! Help me say and do the right things." So, I just listened, (I really did), then asked a few innocuous questions that were not up to my self-image of a good counselor. I quietly said, "I will pray for you."

Dah. Dumb. How trite, how shallow. I knew I was a poor counselor.

Then, one Saturday morning (Ah, no school) a knock came at my door. It was 6:00 in the morning. Not my best hour. It was Carol. With tears in her eyes she, without preamble blurted out that her husband had left her. "He's gone."

I hugged her and said, "Oh, Carol, Carol, I'm so sorry." I took her hands and said through my own tears, "Let me pray for you." She then told me the whole, wretched story of the issues that so often break up a marriage.

We were both exhausted as her voice trailed off and I continued to comfort her. I offered a book* that had helped me a lot through difficult situations and asked if she would like to read it. She tearfully said, "Yes". I said the book had been very helpful to me when I had gone through a difficult situation earlier. "We'll discuss it when you get through reading it."

Two days later she had finished the book and came by to talk. Right off she told me that she particularly enjoyed the chapter entitled, *The Prayer of Relinquishment*. Trusting God and letting go. "It was life changing when I read it," she said quietly.

"Have you ever made a commitment your life to Christ, asked Him to come into your life?" I asked, matching her mood.

"Yes," she said with a big smile, "Yes! I made that step as I was reading the book. I feel so great ever since, I feel so transformed." I was so thrilled and gave her a big hug.

That night I invited Carol to go with me to a Bible study group, a group I discovered just a few days after I arrived in New Hampshire. The group was a warm, loving, supportive group and Bible study. It was perfect for Carol while going through her very difficult personal situation.

She began to grow in her relationship with God. It was inspiring to watch her blossom. Since Roger was still out at sea with the navy, (I dreamt he was going around the world again), I had time to walk Carol through her lonely, sad moments. And, in turn, Carol had a generous spirit of helping me become a better teacher. She and I prayed for her husband to return. She was even able to see how she may have contributed to her husband's unhappiness. That prayer was not immediately answered.

Three years later Roger, now discharged, and I moved west so that he could attend seminary. It was great to be in sunny, warm California. After we found a small apartment and Roger had started grinding out Greek and homiletics classes, I received a surprise note from Carol. It said, "Bud has returned! My response could be nothing but, 'Oh, thank you Lord!

I prayed: "Thank you for letting me be a small part of bringing life and healing and salvation to Carol along the way. There is no greater experience".

* *Beyond Ourselves*, by Katherine Marshall. Wife of Peter Marshall, a Presbyterian pastor and chaplain to the United States Senate.

YOUR STORY

_____
_____
_____
_____

Chapter 28

I'll TAKE SIX, BUT NO MEALS

Roger had retired and had moved back to Lookout Mountain. One day I received a phone call from our pastor's wife. She asked if I could take some Africans (six to be exact) into our home for eight days. My first thought was that eight days is a long time, but my second better thought was "I can do that if they are just sleeping in our home for eight days." She continued to say that the people coming were from French speaking Gabon, on the west coast of Africa. They were coming for their son's wedding. He had just graduated from Vanderbilt University and his fiancé, a member of our church, just finished her psychiatric nurse practitioner training from the same university. This was the first time for the family to visit the United States. I thought I better clarify that I would not be cooking meals. To sleep, yes to eat, no. Cooking three meals a day for eight days seemed a bit over whelming and expensive. Our pastor's wife said, "No, you won't have to cook. Maybe you could give them a cup of coffee in the morning to start the day." "I can do that!"

The day for the wedding party quickly rolled around and, yes, six African's arrived at my door, and at the same time a message on the computer. The message was an inkling that something changed. It read: "The Africans said that the breakfast they liked was coffee, eggs, fruit, bacon and dry cereal." In my mind, I thought, "What happened to just coffee?" Oh, well, I guess I can give them breakfast. The new African friends were very lovely. (Two mothers-one birth mother and the one who raised him, two aunts and a father, really an uncle who raised him.) Only one could speak English!

The English speaker and I of necessity became fast friends. She helped my understanding of what was going on. The afternoon of the first day, in walked our new guests with bags and bags of groceries. The one who spoke English asked if she could rearrange my refrigerator, so they could fit the groceries in. Shock! No one said anything about their cooking in our home.

I ran over to my neighbor, Penny, breathlessly saying, "You'll never believe what is happening in our home. I had to talk to her just for comic relief.

Shortly later there were eleven Africans sitting in my small living room. Later after I reported to Penny, I asked, "How did this happen?" We laughed together, which helped. I went back home and the bride, whom I didn't know, was there. I said to her, "I wasn't planning on people eating here." She proceeded to say, "Thank you, so much." I repeated that I really didn't expect to have people eating in my home. I was feeling very sad for her, but that was the contract. Then a second better thought came, "Okay, God, here is a chance to show your love to these people and help someone out." My third thought was, "But I really don't want to do it! Help!"

As it turned out, the people were very nice and helpful and every morning we greeted each other with a kiss on each cheek. The first few days I kept forgetting to kiss the second cheek and we clumsily kept bumping noses.

I did cook breakfast for our guests and the breakfast time became a very fulfilling occasion. The ladies cooked their other meals and made sure everything was very clean and tidy after each meal. Our conversations each morning and night became a wonderful and happy time. In fact, I was getting to like it, and thought, "I could get used to this." Once I relinquished my rights, God could do His thing. The bride was so overwhelmed with all the family and out of town guests, we even decided to give her relief by taking the family sightseeing around the mountain. They loved it; I loved it and the bride was given a break in her overwhelming schedule.

Now how did God come along the way in a potentially negative situation? Because of having these Africans in our home one of the groomsmen, who was part of the nightly crowd, got into a conversation with my husband. The groomsman turned out to be a Muslim and asked Roger why he changed from engineering to the pastorate. Roger was then able to share with him how he became a Christian at the university and presented the gospel to him.

Another wonderful thing happened. The one woman who could speak English with a French accent broke down and cried the last day at the breakfast table and said how much this time had meant to her and how she felt God's love in our home and said she had not experienced that before. We had a few talks about how she had experienced God in America and how she was so surprised. She read my book which clearly told how I became a Christian and she was touched.

Thank you, Lord, for not letting her see my true feelings on the first day of their arrival. Thank you also for helping to change my attitude so you could come along the way and impact the Africans' lives for your Kingdom.

The French speaking lady also bought three of my books "The Perfect Minister's Wife, Another Book of Fiction" to give to her friends in France. In that book is a clear presentation of how to become a child of God.

Offer hospitality to one another without grumbling. Each one should use whatever gift he has received to serve others, faithfully administering God's grace in its various forms.

1 Peter 4:9,10

YOUR STORY

_____
_____
_____
_____
_____

Chapter 29

WOOD CHIPS

It was Roger's first church after seminary. He was the crisp, new associate pastor, filled with vim and vigor to fulfill his first calling to serve the Lord. Should he be a Billy Graham or a Martin Luther?

The venerable church we were called to was over 300 years old and so was the average age of the small-town congregation. The place was musty with history. The question was: Is there spiritual excitement or even sparkles of life in that congregation? In allf our innocent, wide-eyed, bouncy enthusiasm, we couldn't find a sparkle. "Oh, Lord, how did we get here? Why? How can we help bring this church some spiritual life?" It was more than discouraging. Why are we here? Had we misread the Lord's signals?

Roger, was weary, reaching the point of deciding to leave his ministry after almost two years of that church's stultifying deadness. Maybe he could get a job with IBM and catch people off guard as he spoke of Christ. That would be better than have church people yawn at the mention of the Savior.

"Roger, put your net down on the other side of the boat," came that unmistakable ringing voice. "Joy, you help too."

Nets? Oh, the disciples' nets. And no fish. We get it!

We hung in there. We learned to fish, and we began to see God do amazing things in the lives of those prosaic, weary people.

Here's a great story from those days. It is a remembrance we often chuckle about.

There was a couple in the church who had just become Christians and wanted to follow Christ, no matter what he asked. At that time Roger had been teaching about the curious subject of tithing. This young, attractive, lively couple decided, because the Bible taught it, that they wanted to give ten percent of their income to the Lord's work. But that decision created some difficulty. They had recently bought a new house and they wanted to make the home and the yard look lovely. They had painted the house and purchased some shrubs. All they had to do now was to put woodchips around the shrubs and trees.

The class, and especially this couple, struggled with this new concept of tithing. It especially hit this couple because just then they wanted to buy those woodchips which would perfect their yard.

"Oh, well, we'll start tithing next month." But as the Spirit of God often does with his young, new followers, he wouldn't let them keep up their rationalization.

"We'll start tithing next month." "Seek first the kingdom of God and his righteousness and all these things will be added to you," came the majestic voice. At times Roger had mentioned what Joy's mother often said, "You cannot out give the Lord. You shovel out with your shovel and he shovels back with his and his shovel is bigger than yours."

Finally, after some genuine, inward struggles, George and Barbara decided they would forget the woodchips and be obedient to their Lord. The next Sunday having given their tithes with a heart of obedience, they went home with a mixture delight and some dismay about their scraggly, unimaginative yard. As he got out of the car and walked up their unadorned sidewalk, the neighbors called out, "Hey, George, buddy, how was church? I've been working in the garden and have all these woodchips left over from the truck load I bought. Can you use them?"

George and Barbara looked at each other with broad, knowing grins, "Oh, yes, yes!" he hollered back to the neighbor. "We'd love them. Thanks a lot! You may not know it, but you are an answer to our prayers. Thanks."

They could hardly wait to get to the small group Bible study that evening so they could tell the group about God's faithfulness toward obedience. "Tell them, George, tell them."

In your mind, jump ahead ten years.

We are leading a small group for young couples in another church. They were marvelously young in the faith and full of mind and spirit testing questions. "Yeah, but what's all this about tithing?" shouted one of the young men. Roger, adding some funny details, told them our wood chip story.

One husband, a believer of just a few weeks, nearly exploded, "Wait, wait. That's not really a true story, is it?" We assured him that it was.

"This very week my wife and I had a big argument. We're talking about huge. Our argument was about whether to tithe this week or buy woodchips for yard."

God's mysterious, happy ways are always very interesting. And He knows a lot about gardens.

Your story of God's graciousness.

_____
_____
_____
_____
_____
_____

Chapter 30

OH NO!

Both my husband and I are amazed at how the Lord works in amazing ways in our lives. particularly in the area of finances. I shouldn't be surprised because even when money was tight, o family would still tithe. My mother would say, "Joy, where is your faith?" We shovel out to God, and He shovels back to us, and his shovel is bigger than ours." I'm now 82 years old and I have found that so true.

Both Roger and I have stories to tell about God's amazing faithfulness; so often around money. These stories are quite unique on how God works things out.

Case in point: Roger and I were visiting my brother at the beach in New Jersey. Late one afternoon Roger decided to walk on the beach. As he walked with his feet in the surf, a thought came to his mind. "I haven't gotten in the water yet this vacation, and it is very hot! I have shorts on. Why not jump in and really be refreshed?" He took off his shirt and cap and walked into the water, knee high, waist high, and then came a wave. As he dove into the wave, he heard a loud, strange gurgling sound in his ears. He reached up and one hearing aid was gone. He could never find it in the boiling surf. He frantically put his hand to his other ear. It was there! But would it work after being soaked in salt water? Dejectedly he thought, "There goes $1000 down the drain!" He dried off the remaining hearing aid and put it in his hat for the sun to dry it. He took a short walk and when he came back, he checked the hearing aid. It did not work.

"There goes $2000." He slowly trudged back home thinking, "That was pretty stupid, but there is nothing I can do about it now. Thank God that we have $2000 to get new hearing aids. " When he got back to the cabin, he put the one hearing aid on the bureau with a tiny bit of hope that it might work in the morning. But probably not. Salt water is a killer for electronics.

The next morning, he gave it a try and…it worked! "Wonderful! Now I'm only out $1000." Then a thought came. "Isn't there a two-year warranty on the hearing aids that includes loss?" He looked on line and "yes" there is. But how long had he had the hearing aids? Then with his trusty iPhone he looked back in credit card reports. Oops. He purchased them two years and two weeks ago. A grasping for straws idea came to his mind. "I wonder if I could get by with one hearing aid? Hah. I need two."

Finally, vacation was over, and we went home. It was time to bite the bullet and buy a new hearing aid. He went to Costco's hearing aid center and asked the audiologist about the warranty. "It's just a couple weeks over the two years, could you check to see if it possibly is still good?"
She kindly replied, "A month ago I checked on something like that for my mother. Nope. Two years is the limit.

Roger thought, 'Well, I tried." So, he ordered a new hearing aid and started walking around Costco looking for their famous free samples: cookies, chips, cheese, anything for free. About ten minutes later Roger's cell phone rang. It was the audiologist. She said, "I checked and saw that you purchased your hearing aids with an express card. I remembered that AMEX adds one year to your warranty. You get a free one."

Minus $2000, then $1000, now $0.00. Roger's heart was light. Thank you, Lord.

But that was not all. About a year earlier Roger left his hearing aid remote control at a motel. It was a very helpful thing that would turn the hearing aids on and off and modify the volume. He thought of buying a new one, but they cost around $150. So, he didn't replace it.

Guess what? When the new, free hearing aid came in, it included a remote.

Minus $2000, then $1000, then $0.00 and finally plus $150! What a wonderful gift from God.

"We shovel out and God shovels back in and his shovel is bigger than ours."
Mary Keating

Your story of God's amazing provision

_____
_____
_____
_____

Chapter 31

A ROAD LESS TRAVELED

Almost every morning, Roger and I take a mile and a quarter walk down the craggy, wooded hill behind our home, across the school playground and then down the golf course. Destination? A coffee shop and devotions as we sipped. The coffee isn't as smooth bodied and subtle as Roger's just roasted, freshly ground brew, but for ninety-nine cents what does one expect.

Each summer we would track the steep path to the lush green woods. Of course, there was a quaint, worn, wooden bridge over the small creek that perfected the greeting card, sylvan look.

Each spring, green buds and yellow jasmine bloomed as the morning light shimmered through the trees, which were about to become the cool green foliage and shade of summer. Alas, too quickly, there were the unbelievable colors of autumn, gold, orange and red. Then reluctantly as we headed out for a coffee in winter, the trees were laden with their crystal dazzle and bowed down with winter's snow.

We are never bored on our walks, together down to the little coffee shop. However, one day I chattered on to Roger, "Let's do something new. Let's break the routine and walk the new sidewalk the city has just completed. We can get our coffee at the grocery store. It's three times as far and is not as lovely as our walk through our woods, but for some reason I felt it will be fun."

We arrived at the quaint looking, Germanic, Hansel and Gretel grocery store. (I should have worn my dirndl and Roger his Tyrolean lederhosen.) We bought our coffee and got comfortable on the antique rockers on the front porch. As we began to rock, careful not to slosh the steaming coffee, a woman came out of the store and headed for her car. She had the brisk, healthy look of a professional golfer.

Spontaneously and cheerfully I called over to her, "Are you a professional golfer?" She laughed and said, "My husband would think that was funny. I can't play golf or tennis." I plunged on, "Well, you look every bit a professional sports person to me." "Sorry," was her reply, "My main activity is writing for the local Mountain Mirror about what is going on around Lookout Mountain. I have a regular column with my picture on it."

"Oh, I knew I'd recognized you. Happy to meet you." An uncensored thought flashed into my head, and I blurted out without thinking, "I just published a book about the fun and foibles that result from being a minister's wife. Meet Roger, the minister." I was a little chagrined by my boldness, but out it came.

As any southern, gentle lady would say, she responded, "I'd love to read it. If you drop it off at my house, I'll write a review for my next column. And local authors are always interesting."

Wow! My book was hot off the press and now I was to be reviewed. I had been wondering how I could introduce my book to the community.

With walk, coffee and rocking chairs over, we headed home at a brisker pace. I pulled a copy of my brand-new book from the just opened box and headed over to my new friend's house. My mother taught me to be assertive, but not pushy. I was being a bit assertive. Would her review be positive?

It was. The columnist's kind words launched my new career. A local shop took copies and featured them in their window. The drugstore and local restaurant ask for copies too. Would talk shows and a national tour come next? Probably not. But maybe some churches?

I had never seen that wonderful woman who launched my fragile career before or since.

I wondered. Had God changed the path we usually took just so we might meet that nice columnist?

What do you think?

Your Story of God's guidance.

_____

_____

_____

_____

Chapter 32

BUT FOR THIS VERY HOUR...

I always hated my middle name. Esther. I never told anyone that the reason for my hating that dreaded middle name was because there was a girl in one of my high school classes with that same terrible name. She was just a frizzy headed blond and was skinny and dressed like an old lady and stuff like that. Good bye middle name. How's that for maturity?

On the other hand, I've always loved the Old Testament story about the, oh wow, knock 'em dead, beautiful Esther. Way back then when kings and queens oversaw what was going on, Queen Vashti shirked off the King's command for her to come at once to *his* opulent, drunken garden party that he was throwing for his leading generals and governors. (Didn't that not-so-bright king remember she was giving her own party for the ladies? She also wasn't very excited about being the object of dozens of drunken men's leers.)

The king's courtyard had been decorated with beautifully woven white and blue linen hangings, fastened by purple ribbons to silver rings that were embedded in marble pillars. Gold and silver couches stood on a mosaic pavement of marble, mother-of-pearl and other costly stones. Drinks were served in gold goblets and there was an abundance of royal wine. Those who wished could have as much wine as they pleased. (I haven't been to a royal party in years. Actually never.)

The king wanted to show off to all his guy friends his beautiful queen. *After all, she was the fairest in the land.* And already this six-month-long bash was losing its steam. But the queen refused to come. The king decided right then, with his advisors' counsel, to get another wife. "What if the word gets out that the queen refused her husband's order. All the wives might begin doing that!" It was as simple as that. Get a new queen!

After an extended search throughout the kingdom, Esther was chosen. She was, by all measures, in form and face, the most exquisite of the young virgins in the empire. She was soaked in ritual baths of oil of myrrh for six months. She was dabbed for another six months with Hermes' perfumes and then creamed with Channel cosmetics. (You can read the first telling of this epic story in the Old Testament book called, not surprisingly, *Esther.*)

However, she had no idea what a life changing task for that Jewish community God had for her to do "Esther had come to this royal position for such a time as this."

Not long ago, way after my namesake Queen Esther became part of God's epochal story, I met another exquisite beauty in the Middle East whom God had in mind to affect our current events. This attractive woman in her early forties had been called by God to leave the U.S. and go to a Muslim country to work with a non-governmental organization (NGO). Their ministry was to provide water purification equipment and blankets for refugees. She was a person one wouldn't have expected to find in such a difficult place. Summers were 120 degrees in the shade and with lots of dust. Air conditioning would go off two or three times a day with no telling when its minimally cool breeze would come back on.

She was a perfect size petite and very feminine, a refreshing contrast to the darker skin and brown eyes of the mid-eastern women who were often covered by a black burka. While in her new country she unexpectedly became friends with the niece of a very important leader of that country and through attending various parties and events she became friends with many government officials.

Jump ahead a few years to a Christian Family Camp our Entrust staff put on for men, women and children who had come to faith in Christ from the Muslim world. It was a yearly retreat where families came to be safe, learn about their faith, sing, worship and just have fun. About 200 people were to be there. Children's ministries were planned, Bible teachers were ready and fun activities were in place.

A day before the camp began a phone call came. "The man from India who was to lead our children's work will not be let into the country." Whaaat? An agent at the airport said he must have a visa and invitation before they would let him enter the country. But that had all been checked out earlier. He didn't need all that, but that passport agent was determined our children's director was *not* coming into his country. He kept demanding: "Get your suitcase from the luggage carousel now! You will be sent out of the country on the next flight out!"

Cleverly, the friends who were with him at the airport said they just couldn't find the suitcase that was supposed to be circulating on the baggage carousel. They knew if they picked it up, our children's director for the camp would be gone.

Emergency phone calls were made to our *Queen Esther*. This petite, blue eyed blond lady who was also helping with our family camp when told the story, called her friend the Minister of Interior for the country. The word was passed on to the passport agent that he was about to receive a phone call from the Minister of the Interior. "The Minister will approve our Mr. Mumar's entry." The Agent scoffed and shouted, "Find that suit case, now."

In a few minutes the Minister of the Interior called our not so friendly luggage agent and visa checker and told him to let this man into the country, at once! The suitcases that mysteriously couldn't be found on the carousel appeared. And *voila* the visa was stamped, and our friend was admitted into the country.

Incredible. What a blessing he was to our family conference.

I kept thanking my blond, *Queen Esther*. In response she would shyly smile. She admitted to me that she was excited that God had used her and her relationship with people in high places for God's work at a time like this.

"Then the king asked her, "What do you wish, Queen Esther? What is your request? I will give it to you, even if it is half the Kingdom!" Esther 5:3

YOUR STORY OF SEEING GOD'S GREAT TIMING:

_____
_____
_____
_____
_____

Chapter 33

NOW WHAT?

I have always been amazed in my life how God shows up in ways I never expected or could have created if I tried. I had just graduated from college and like every graduate wondered what in the world I was going to do for my life's work. I was overwhelmed. Here my parents had just paid out thousands of dollars for my education and now it was time to produce.

I had two potential jobs that were offered to me: Christian Education Director of the New England Fellowship and Christian Education Director of a church in the small town of Carmel, Illinois. When I prayed about these two possibilities neither of them triggered my imagination. In fact, they made me feel depressed. But since God had only given me these two options, one of them must be the job of choice. Then one day a third choice came along the way in the form of an older friend who came to visit my brother. He said to me, "Joy why don't you come on Young Life Staff."

Young Life is an organization that works with high school students. I knew a little about Young Life but didn't think I liked their approach. He said, "Well, pray about it." I said I would and I just prayed a quick prayer, so I could tell him I had prayed. He came back the next week and asked, "Did you pray about Young Life and what do you think." I told him, "Yes I had prayed but I'm really not interested." He then proceeded to ask me another question. "Why don't you come out to the Young Life Ranch in Colorado and counsel for a week: You can go along on the bus full of high school kids and be one of the chaperones". Now that rang a bell in my head. No long-term commitment and a free trip to Colorado. All this could happen before I needed to decide about those other two job opportunities. My motives were not pure, but I knew Young Life was not for me.

So, within a week I was on the bus to Colorado. Stupidly, I didn't plan about money for meals along the trip. But God knew. My brother who came to see me off, handed me an envelope. Would you believe in that envelope was just enough money to cover my food expenses on my way to the ranch.

Was I in for a surprise. From the time I arrived at the ranch and became a counselor, I fell in love with Young Life and its whole approach to high school students. Not only was the ranch incredible but to have the privilege of leading some of my cabin girls to Christ was beyond, beyond!

As I learned more about Young Life's approach, the more I wanted to be on Young Life staff. The job fit me like a glove. I thought I was just going on this trip to see Colorado and be on a real live ranch, but God was working out his purposes, "Along the Way."

For three years I worked for Young Life in Baltimore, Maryland before marrying Roger. Little did I know then that God was preparing me for the ministry in all our churches. In our first two churches Roger was hired to work with youth and young adults. I felt so at home doing just what God had trained me to do in Young Life. God's ways are so, so good!

"Lord be my rock of safety, the stronghold that saved me. For the honor of your name lead me and guide me."

Your Story of God's leading.

_____
_____
_____
_____

Chapter 34

A SUNBEAM

Our memories are curious things.

What we can't recall is as impressive as those thoughts we can't get rid of. Remember a final exam you studied for all night *(Your score on this test would constitute a third of your grade!)* and you couldn't remember the most important answer?

Or a youthful song like: *Marzy Dotes and Dozy Dotes,* or school yells (Go, Tigers, go!) are all packed indelibly in some obscure cranny of our brains. But we can bring them back at the most unexpected times and circumstances and still not remember our spouse's birthday.

Well, singing was very much a part of my family's experiences and traditions. I used to think it was normal for all families to sing together. But, no.

My first memory of singing a searching song, actually it was loaded with pathos, was when I was two. So cute, so dimply with blond curls. I went wandering through our huge house singing the only song I knew, "Happy Birfday to You" and then called out with heartbreaking pathos, "Mama, Mama". I couldn't find her in our three stories, Victorian home. (From my tiny height, it was scary, and crawling up our long flights of stairs took all my skill.) Mama. Happy Birfday.

Yes, of course, you're supposed to get a tear in your eye. I always do, even now, when I tell the story. Mama always appeared, picked me up and hugged and kissed me. That was so good.

But all singing was not pathos. Some was spiritual and uplifting. The next memory I have of singing was as a soloist, age seven, at the Rescue Mission where my father was Director. Every Sunday afternoon, circa 1943, there was a chapel service for the men who had come to the mission for help. They were, as many were during the depression, struggling with alcoholism, unemployment, broken homes, or disabilities. My father must have thought this was a good place for his daughter of seven to have her debut--and surely touch the hearts of the struggling men. I pipped clearly, as only a cute little ringlet-ed child could, "Jesus wants me for a sunbeam." (It was heartbreaking. Eat your heart out Shirley Temple.) I remember, even then, hoping God would through my singing speak to all those sad looking, defeated men. Maybe someday in heaven someone *will* come up to me and say, "I remember your sunbeam song. That song helped me get things going again." Dad would say at the end of my little chirpy song, "And a little child shall lead them."

Another great singing memory includes my own and extended family. We always sang when we got together, be it at a Christmas or a Thanksgiving bash, or just an anniversary or festive day. It was mostly hymns that we sang, but we easily lapsed into any tune (silly was good) that we knew. We would always sing--after the first verse--in glorious, four-part harmony. After a resplendent Thanksgiving meal, we would continue to sit around the huge, now cleared, table and sing, after just the title was announced, through the whole hymn book. We knew all the words, without looking, and sang most of the verses.

If that was good, and we were all laughing, someone would give the first three notes of a hymn or song and see if anyone could the remember the whole lyric. Someone always guessed. "OK, try singing only the first two notes of a song." Do dah. We were usually as clever in knowing the hymn with just the two notes. More laughter and joshing. Of course, being competitive we would laugh and race to see who was the cleverest at guessing. I imagined that all Christian families did something similar until I discovered that not only could people not guess a hymn with just two notes, they didn't sing hymns at all. (After the Austrian Trapp Family Singers, there was us.)

And thus, began my singing career. I sang in trios in church when in high school. That led to college chorales and church solos. From those family experiences there was always a hymn in my mind, if only to hum, that spoke to that situation and brought comfort or expressed a strong feeling. When it was cloudy, out came a little chorus (often just a ditty) I learned in church

"Sing and smile and pray, sing the clouds away,

When you sing and smile and pray, you'll sing the clouds away"

Or perhaps, "Heavenly Sunshine". Every Sunday School kid of our era knew it.

Heavenly sunshine, heavenly sunshine, flooding my soul with glory divine,

Heavenly sunshine, heavenly sunshine, Hallelujah, Jesus is mine.

There were so many good feelings connected with those songs they always picked up my spirits and immediately make me feel better on a dull, dreary day. Still do.

Then, when days are more serious, there are the words from such majestic hymns as,

> *Great is thy faithfulness oh, God my Father!*
> *There is no shadow of turning with Thee*
> *Thou changest not. Thy compassions they fail not.*
> *As thou hast been Thou forever wilt be.*

Then, strangely, there have been the times when I felt overwhelmed and the song, "Onward Christian Soldiers" would come bounding into my mind and happily keep me moving forward.

There were situations when I wanted to speak for Christ and I was fearful to do so, but the song "Lift High the Cross, the love of Christ proclaim," would seep into my brain and encourage me and refresh my soul.

Yes, of course, I took voice lessons in college and began to sing in the choirs. There were frequent solos in my home church which gave me a whole repertoire for every life situation.

I saw God along the way when he gave me a family that sang, gave me songs that would well up in my mind in every life situation of joy, wonder or hardship. What a gift!

So, start singing.

"If there is no joy there is a leak in your Christianity somewhere." Billy Sunday

YOUR STORY

_____

_____

_____

_____

Chapter 35

JUST IN TIME

There are things in life that bring out fear in me.

Driving in large, unfamiliar cities is one of them. This horrifying fear showed itself rather abruptly when my daughter, Kathleen, asked me to pick up my husband at Chicago's O'Hare airport. She had dropped him off and I had expected her to pick him up. However, this day she was very tired. "Mom, could you please pick Dad up?" No, no. My fear began to take control. I begged her to pick him up. "Honey, please pick your father up." My fear thought, "If I get lost I'll never return. I'll be off to Wisconsin. There is so much traffic and no way on those busy interstate highways to turn around except on ramps that lead nowhere I know".

All my pleading was to no avail. But to comfort me, Kat gave me her smart phone which had Google Maps on it. That little person in her cell phone would direct me all the way to the airport. With great confidence, Kat said, "Place the phone on the seat and do not touch it. It will speak and tell you how to get to O'Hare."

I was feeling a little bit better, but not much better.

So out to the car I went with my shaky new confidence. I started on the roads out of Wheaton with confidence. The sweet, little voice from the smart phone didn't give directions to the interstate. "Oh, well, I knew those turns anyway." I turned on to the dreaded highway with a little less confidence. I was flying down the crowded highway at sixty-five miles an hour waiting for the next command. None came.

I was now thirty minutes into the trip. At this point I started praying, "Oh Lord, please be with me I'm now on my way to the airport and I don't know how to get there." I drove for about fifteen minutes more. I read all the exit signs, and nothing suggested, Airport.

There was a sign "Milwaukee" at a big right-hand curve. Somewhere in my head I remembered my daughter mentioning Milwaukee or Wisconsin, so I took the big curve. She also said I'd see all kinds of signs to the Airport. Wrong! Not a sign and nothing familiar only three huge signs with strange city names on them. I had to choose one.

At this point, I cried out to the Lord to please help me. At that moment the little cell phone next to me said, "In 50 feet turn right." I turned right. And there were those blessed signs saying, "Airport." Every turn was clear as could be after that.

The next challenge was finding my husband in that massive airport. I dutifully, cautiously followed the signs to Delta. There he stood. I jumped out, gave him a hug and said, "YOU DRIVE HOME!"

Your Story of God helping you when you felt alone or not ready for what was ahead.

_____
_____
_____
_____
_____

Chapter 36

IT WAS MORE THAN THE OIL

Our son, Tim, a typical college senior, dreaded his final exams, but he also knew the celebrations were going to be great around graduation. He knew he'd feel proud and was somewhat confident because he'd always done well academically. We were already planning a trip to Wheaton College looking forward to meeting all the smiling students and happy parents (no more tuition bills). I was planning what to wear for graduation. The phone rang. It was one of the house parents where Tim lived. There was no "Hello," no pleasantries. "Tim is really sick. I think you need to get here right away!" She continued with a rapid-fire diagnosis. "His throat is white and has pus in it. He can't open his mouth or even eat or drink. Worse still, his temperature is 104. He may have to go to the hospital.

For a houseparent to call at all was unusual, but there was a very serious note in her voice. I assured her we would be there as quickly as we could. However, Roger, then a pastor of a large congregation, had to make some quick arrangements. Had to find someone to preach on Sunday and, of course, every pastor for miles around was already booked or on vacation. Then there was a wedding rehearsal and dinner and the wedding on Saturday. That had been in the works for months. The bride and her family would be crushed, confused and possibly angry. None of that mattered. What mattered was Tim.

We went into a frenzy of packing, grabbing essentials from our closets and dressers while making lots of phone calls to be sure everything at home and church continue to function for as long as we were gone. For how long?

From our peaceful home, we fled to Illinois, often not quite within the speed limit, concerned only for Tim. Wasn't there a campus doctor? Surely a nurse. The school wasn't in the back country. Of course, I prayed even when it was my turn to drive. Will we ever get there? "Lord, what was going on? You know we love and care for our only son. We know you love him. Please heal him." My mind and the car were in overdrive. I was practically shouting at God going seventy miles an hour. Roger dozed off.

Physically and emotionally exhausted, we arrived on campus and went to Tim's room. We had been there other times but for happier occasions. I wasn't prepared for what I saw. Tim was in bed, pale and fevered. I touched his very warm head and gently brushed back his hair. "Tim, it's Mom and Dad. Can we get you some water?" He barely opened his eyes as though looking at a bright light. Though he tried, he couldn't ever sip the water. He dozed off.

Roger, having been on more than one parishioner's sick calls, had brought a small vial of olive oil. Jesus' brother, James, wrote eons ago, "Is any one of you sick? He should call the elders of the church to pray over him and anoint him with oil in the name of the Lord. And the prayer offered in faith will make the sick person well; the Lord will raise him up."

So, Roger lightly traced a cross on Tim's forehead with his oiled finger, we prayed for healing. Moments after we finished praying, Tim opened his mouth wide, coughed a bit and carefully sat up. We quickly brought in some soft and warm food. Without any help, he was able to get up and go to the bathroom. The next day he went to his classes and took all his makeup exams. He was so pale, but his skyrocketed fever was gone. Yes, God had answered our prayers. We were a happy, thankful and joyful family.

We later found out that what Tim had was a disease which had been prevalent during World War II. Tim had been skateboarding in a concrete drainage ditch that had had sewage run through it. He either fell and scraped himself or drank some polluted water and thus got trench mouth.

Your Story of God's healing.

_____
_____
_____
_____
_____
_____

Chapter 37

FAMILY FORGIVENESS

A long time ago Roger and I worked with high school and college students for many years. We had high school and college students in our home almost day and night. We loved the age group and knew how to relate to them. So, when Roger's mother, who had a child late in life and was struggling with his teenage antics, asked if we could host him for the summer. We gladly and almost joyfully said yes, "Send him on."

Bob came and all our expectations of impacting his life for good, having him enjoy our youth group of eighty kids, and maybe even becoming a Christian didn't happen. I always had related well with high school kids and had previously been able to get along with the worst of them…*but* that summer with Bob I was put to a big test and failed. Bob would use our car which we cautiously loaned to him and ran it out of gas and left it for us to come and get the car. He thought it was funny when I wasn't looking to give beer and cigarettes to Tim and Kathy, our five and eight-year-old children. Bob would do inappropriate things with the girls in our youth group. He would swear at me regularly. I planned to love him through it all, but anger rose up in me and I really grew to hate him. I was so mad I couldn't wait until he went home. I prayed for love, but love eluded me. He finally left after two months. Yea!

But guess where, a short time later, Roger decided we needed to go on vacation for two weeks? We didn't have money for a real vacation, so we went to visit his parents... and Bob! It was at that point that I began praying, "Oh God, please give me a love for Randy." We arrived at Roger's parents' home and though I tried, I could not work up any positive feelings towards him.

One time the family decided to go shopping. I told them I would stay at home. They left, and I got on my knees to pray and work thru my anger. I cried out to God, "I can't love him. Please help me." "Love your neighbor as yourself" repeated itself in my head. I remembered a few years earlier having learned a process for working through forgiveness when forgiveness was hard. The Christian teacher suggested three steps:

Step 1. Write down a list of the offender's faults.
That was easy. I wrote pages.

Step 2. Write a list of your own offenses regarding the offender. I thought I'd acted well...but *it was* an act. I began writing down my faults (A fairly short list).

Step 3: Purpose in your heart to ask forgiveness for the part where you failed.

That would be hard, but I was going to do it. It was an act of obedience. That night at dinner I was going to put a little present beside Bob's plate and even laugh at his jokes.

The process was emotionally exhausting, so I laid down for a nap before everyone got home from shopping and dinner preparations began. During my nap I had a dream that began to give me a bit of sympathy for Bob.

At dinner that night I acted lovingly towards Bob, though I still had plenty of negative feelings. Fake it till you make it. In our dinner conversation, my mother-in-law (Bob's mom) happened to mention that when she couldn't sleep at night, she would get up and read. I commented, "I never wake up at night."

That night I had another dream about Randy. I realized he was born when his father was forty-nine years old and that he grew up with perfectionist parents who were very hard on him. A loving, caring feeling welled up in me… a deeper understanding of why he needed unconditional love. I woke up with warm, sympathetic feelings toward Bob.

Contrary to what I had said during dinner about never waking up at night, I woke up. I couldn't go back to sleep. So, I got up and went out into the living room. A moment later Bob walked into the room. We sat and talked for hours. I asked him for forgiveness. He said, "Oh don't worry about it."

God answered my prayers. Ever since then I've had warm feelings for Bob. It certainly wasn't because he changed. He didn't for a long time.

Bob is now a fun, alive Christian who sings and plays the guitar for worship at his church. The Lord is good and His ways past finding out.

"And we know that God works all things together for good for those who love Him and are called according to his purposes."

Your story of forgiveness.

_____
_____
_____
_____

Chapter 38

ACHTUNG!

Exchange students. There were nine!

German, Russian, Uzbek, Mexican, Argentinean, and Austrian. None were planned for--except the two girls from Argentina. Usually high school exchange students were placed in nice upper class, suburban homes where all went well and there was plenty of extra help. Of course, there were always creepy times when the father of the household developed glittering, lusty eyes and became a little frisky and friendly with a pretty, young, naïve, international, student. Or, there were the last-minute sponsoring families who changed their minds. *"Honey, we're so sorry. Our very rich Aunt Matilda just died, and we have to go to her funeral in Hawaii."*

One afternoon Roger and I received a call when our local school's Student Placement Director--out of desperation--called us. Pleadingly, she said, "Could you help us out? I'm desperate. Could you, by any chance, take a lovely, exchange student from Germany? Her name is Gretchen."

Thus, just like that, with only my simple "Um, OK" we were the parents of a very lovely teenager from Germany. (Oh, just the week before I was, feeling so free. Our two children had just left for college).

Since Roger was busy being a pastor all day--counseling the broken and sad among us--and busy teaching the Bible and producing sermons, I naturally would be the one to see that this new, academically inquisitive student, with all the strangeness for her being in a new country, would become acclimated to our culture and ways.

I found it fun to entertain the *fraulein*, and to explain to her our own peculiar, cultural customs. Also, when her school would be on a break I could take her with me to see America the Beautiful or at least Tennessee. She really received the insider's view! I was a shameless diplomat for the local Chamber of Commerce. Happily, Gretchen was a great traveler, and each city or town's welcoming sign evoked a cheer of excitement. Each new vista even began looking great to me, even though I had seen them many times.

Gretchen was in our home for the school year. It turned out it was fun having her around our empty-nest home.

I prayed that God would use her time with us and for her to discover the love of Christ and commit her life to Him.

"So, what would you like to see in the United States?" "I would Like to visit California, New York, Texas, and see the Grand Canyon. "Do you realized how long it would take to get to California?" When I told her, she looked at me in amazement and say, "Ach du lieber, I had no idea."

Well, over the months of her stay she and I, and sometimes Roger, did get to Washington and Florida. We also visited our daughter in the Chicago area. Then there was a trip to my childhood home in New Jersey, and, of course, to New York City. "Wow!"

Happily, there was a youth group at our church that warmly welcomed our attractive, bright, charming, blond teen, with a fascinating, non-southern accent. It was a win/win encounter for all.

All of the surprises and excitement of a new teenager's discoveries finally wound down to the last two weeks of her time in America. Roger and I had to attend a pastoral conference one weekend prior to her leaving. I called a good friend to see if she could house Gretchen for a few days. "Sure." Emily graciously said.

We were off, and too quickly back home, from our exhilarating conference.

We burst back into the house to find Gretchen slowly and reluctantly packing her suitcase getting ready to leave the States in the next few days. I poked my head into her room to say something fun and how we would miss her when I noticed a beautiful sweater neatly folded on top of her suitcase. I had never seen it before. Was it to be a surprise thank you for me? "Oh, where did you get such a lovely sweater?" I asked innocently.

"Oh, Beth gave it to me a few weeks ago," she said not looking up. An alarm went off in my head. *A $100 sweater? Almost brand new?* She seemed a little flushed by my questions. I also felt guilty about my intuition that she had stolen it--and quickly dismissed the thought. She didn't have a lot of money, but....

So, after about an hour of pondering and prayer, I did what all mothers of teenagers do, I called the mother of the seemingly generous girl, and said, "Hi, we're back! Had a wonderful conference. Oh, and be sure and thank your daughter for giving Gretchen such a beautiful sweater."

The mother paused for a long moment, "What sweater?" I described it to her. "My daughter doesn't have any sweater like that." Sadly, I wasn't surprised by her answer.

Where could she have gotten such a sweater, I wondered?

I was having a Sherlock Holmes moment. Emily's daughters wore those sweaters all the time and sweet, lovely Gretchen had just spent a weekend there. "Emily. Hi. Would you please ask your daughter if she is missing any sweaters?" Within the hour she called back to say that indeed a sweater was missing.

I expressed my sincere regrets and said that I'd get back to her.

Now what? How can I use for good this unfortunate leave-taking event in Gretchen's life?

Emily and I were on the phone again collaborating on a plan. After I talked with Gretchen, I was to take her over to Emily's to return the sweater and apologize. Emily would then ask why she would steal from their daughter when they were gracious enough to have her stay at their home while we were gone.

Of course, Gretchen cried (along with the rest of us) and asked for forgiveness. She returned the sweater.

That night was the perfect time for me to talk with Gretchen about her relationship with God. It was good timing for me to share with her about a relationship with God. She cried, I explained to her about God's love and forgiveness. We prayed and hugged.

Gretchen left the next day after giving extravagant thanks and appreciation to Roger and me, and for her time with us.

She would keep in touch.

And hopefully, she would be taking a new faith with her.

And, yes, she did keep in touch over the years...but that's another story.

YOUR STORY

_____
_____
_____
_____

Chapter 39

GOD'S AMAZING KINDNESS

My husband, Roger, was a pastor for thirty-six years when we hit some hard pockets of disgruntled parishioners, a difficult thing for any pastor and wife to go through. But it is not an unknown phenomenon for most pastors in people ministry. When these difficult times hit, you examine yourselves to see "if there be any wicked way in your life." We knew we were not perfect followers of Jesus, but the unhappiness of some of our members was beyond what was really going on in the church. But there it was: conflict staring us in the face. It finally rose to a fevered pitch until one unhappy person wrote a forty-page paper against my husband and read it at an elders' meeting with my husband sitting there.

How emotionally devastating it was for my very diligent, faithful husband. It was enough to bring him to tears as that night he related to me what had gone on. I do not remember ever seeing him cry before, but I did that night.

But we serve a very gracious God. An amazing thing "happened" as Roger walked out of that meeting as low as he ever been. God, in his love for his hurting child, had prepared a wonderful gift for him. A few days before, the deacons had met, not knowing anything about the special elders meeting. They had written a resolution of thanksgiving and appreciation for his ten years of ministry with the church. It had been written with calligraphy and beautifully framed. One of the deacons, a physician from England was to give it to Roger. He did not think there was any rush to present it. He was leaving for England the next day. But he told Roger that something made him know he should give it that evening. He waited over an hour in the hall outside the elder's room until the meeting was over. He didn't know why, but he knew he had to give it to Roger before he left for England. This is what it said:

RESOLUTION

Whereas, through the guidance of the Holy Spirit and the will of God, Roger K. Gulick was called to minister to the congregation of First Presbyterian Church, and

Whereas, he has been faithful to his call to teach with inspiration, knowledge, integrity and ability, and

Whereas his vision for a biblically knowledgeable church has been enhanced by his presence, and

Whereas growth in numbers and depth has occurred under his leadership, and

Whereas he continually challenges us to live a life Coram Deo for our personal and corporate good.

BE IT RESOLVED, that we acknowledge with grateful appreciation his presence with us and guidance for us, through the grace of God's holy will.

Is that not just another amazing, gracious illustration of kindness from our heavenly Father the very night Roger was going through one of the hardest moment in ministry.?

Your story of God's gracious, loving dealing with you.

Chapter 40

LITTLE DID I KNOW…

Little did I know when my four-year-old son Timmy got sick on a Sunday morning (a morning when our family usually went full speed ahead and we certainly couldn't be late, since my husband was the pastor) that God had something really good in mind.

Easter Sunday is not a good day to get sick. I was disappointed. Why did my son have to get sick on Easter Sunday morning? But there we were. So, I decided to take full advantage of our sudden extra time together. "I'll do a special Easter church service just for the two of us." I wanted the emphasis of our special time together to be the love of God for us, his wonderful plan for us and how Easter was the center of all that.

As we looked at the Easter story, in children's language, and what Jesus did for us on the cross, and what an amazing thing the resurrection was, something unusual was happening. Timmy said he wanted to become a Christian and give his life to God. Having been a Christian Education major at Wheaton college, I knew that young children will often say whatever they think will please their parents. I had showed Timmy that the Bible teaches that we are to respond to

God's love by asking Christ to come into his life to be with him forever. I tried to show him that this was not a simple thing to do. But Timmy pursued the idea of wanting to become a Christian. So, we prayed together and asked Christ to come live in Timmy. He was so excited! The next day he went up and down the street in our neighborhood and told everyone he could, that he had become a Christian. I thought that was a bit unusual.

About a month later we went up to New Jersey to visit my mother. The first thing Timmy said to her was, "Guess what Grandma, I became a Christian." I was beginning to think maybe this child-like decision was for real. As the years and decades went by he never wavered in that decision, well, not very much.

Twenty-seven years later we received a card from our thirty-one-year-old son.

6-4-95

Dear Mom and Dad,

In a class this morning, our teacher encouraged us to write and thank the person(s) who led us to Christ. So, I'm writing you, Mom, and you, Dad. You two not only prepared the soil and planted the seed, but your fertilized and fostered much of the growth that our Father worked in me. Thank you so, so much for your love, prayers, and guidance through all these thirty plus years. I love y'all and pray for you, almost daily. You make a son proud to be your son.

With love,

Tim

Hooray! God even used a child's sick day and play church to accomplish His purposes.

Tim and his wife Annette have been involved training youth leaders, first in Latin American countries for over fifteen years and in the last few years they are training youth leaders all over the world.

Being a Christian is more than just an instantaneous conversion. It is a daily process whereby you grow to be more and more like Christ. Billy Graham

Your story of God doing something wonderful in your life when "little did you know" what the result would be.

_____
_____
_____
_____
_____
_____

ABOUT THE AUTHOR

Joy Gulick has been a pastor's wife for fifty-four years. She grew up in the Northeast and has lived most of her adult life in the Southeast. She graduated from Wheaton College and worked on Young Life Staff for three years. After her husband retired from the pastorate, together they began to pastor missionaries around the world with Entrust, a mission agency that grows leaders for growing churches. Her first book was a humorous, true story of life as a pastor's wife: The Perfect Minister's Wife: Another Book of Fiction.

Made in the USA
Lexington, KY
17 November 2018